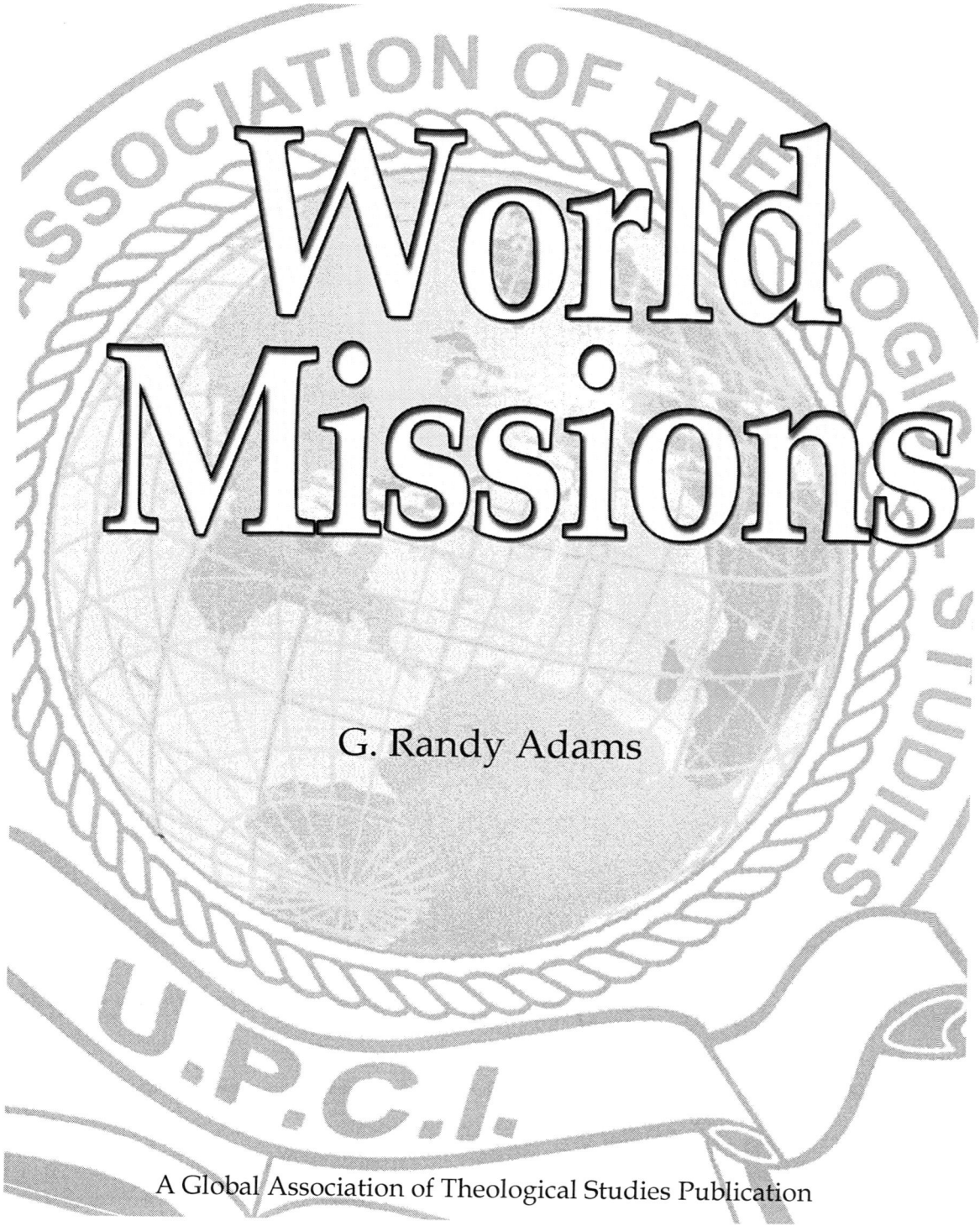

World Missions

G. Randy Adams

A Global Association of Theological Studies Publication

GATS Edition
© 2015 United Pentecostal Church International

Library of Congress Cataloging-in-Publication Data

Adams, G. Randy, 1953-
  World missions / G. Randy Adams. -- GATS Edition.
     pages cm
  "A Global Association of Theological Studies publication."
  ISBN 978-0-7577-4424-2
  1. Missions. I. Title.
  BV2061.3.A33 2015
  266--dc23
                              2015025532

Global Missions
gratefully acknowledges
Landmark Tabernacle
Denver, Colorado
Dannie Hood and Billy Hale, pastors
and its donation of $5000
to fund the production and
translation of
World Missions
by G. Randy Adams

Contents

Foreword

The many daunting challenges of the world's mission fields today can at times be absolutely overwhelming to those laboring to "preach the gospel to every creature." This has often been due to inadequate direction for the missionary and poor preparation for the realities of the field. With an eagerness to fulfill their calling quickly, first-time missionaries arrive on the field and plunge into the work. But in spite of great personal sacrifice and much effort, the end results have been less than productive. As a result, they lose focus, become discouraged, and leave missions. However, with properly trained missionaries, our mission fields can be producing strong, indigenous churches throughout the world that are spiritually alive, robust, and able to overcome every difficulty.

Missionary G. Randy Adams's personal passion, clear insight, and comprehensive approach in this study series, *World Missions*, has produced a tremendous missions resource. Its focus is multilayered. It is a discussion of missions from the sending church's perspective, from the outgoing missionary's burden and calling, and from the receiving church's goals and needs. With a strong scriptural foundation, accurate statistical data, and inspiring personal experience, Missionary Adams has blended a wide-ranging array of information into one powerful world missions study. Every North American pastor and minister of the supporting church needs to read and understand this course. Every potential missionary from every part of the world should read these lessons carefully. Throughout the world, national leaders, pastors, and ministers working hand in hand with resident missionaries should read these lessons as they will help them to fully understand the ministry of the missionary.

A major facet of this ministry is to see the "receiving" church transformed into a "sending" church. Too often, there is a mentality of always "receiving," and this must be reversed so that the work of God can be expanded beyond the borders of the national church. Global missions is not just a duty; it is a mandate from the Lord Jesus. The church exists for the cause of worldwide missions. Without an effective missions witness, the church cannot please the Lord.

Missionary Adams is a field-tested and proven missionary in the countries of Togo and Benin. He immediately began language instruction when he received his personal call to missions, prior to arriving on site. Once there, he gave himself wholeheartedly to the work and to the people of Togo and Benin, launching evangelistic outreach and establishing a strong church for Jesus Christ. Laboring in the sub-Saharan climate of West Africa, the Adams family continued to lead effectively the once-struggling church of Togo to an atmosphere of power, revival, outstanding growth, and spiritual victory.

He also served as a member of Africa Aflame, which is evangelizing and training souls through the printed page. I count it a great privilege to have worked with both him and his wife Carolyn. They are true Christians and outstanding missionaries of the first order. In 2014, he was appointed as my successor as the regional director of UPCI missions in Africa.

The victorious, vibrant church will be able to accomplish this great mission if it follows the biblical approach to evangelizing the world that is found in Randy Adams's study. If you desire to understand the work of missions around the world better, this course will be a tremendous blessing and will benefit you immensely. Instead of "mission impossible," we will agree with this writer, it is "MISSION POSSIBLE!" Enjoy these great lessons on world missions, and be assured that you too are a part of God's big missions plan.

Jerry R. Richardson
Former Regional Director, Africa
United Pentecostal Church International

Introduction

According to the Population Reference Bureau, the world's estimated population stood at 7,238,184,000 in 2014. Every minute, 273 babies are born. Every twenty-four hours adds 392,714 people to our planet. Even considering the mortality rate, the world's population increases by 86,581,000 people every year. PRB projects the 2050 population will be 9,683 billion. (*prb.org/pdf14/2014-world-population-data-sheet_ eng.pdf*, accessed December 3, 2014). This calls for a united effort in world evangelism from the "whole church." It requires a focus on principles that really yield the greatest results. This will ensure that the church planted cross-culturally will stand the test of time, temptation, and trial. The textbook you now hold will serve as a guide along the way.

William Booth, the founder of the Salvation Army, once remarked, "Most Christian ministries would like to send their recruits to Bible college for four to five years. I would like to send our recruits to hell for five minutes. That would do more than anything else to prepare them for a lifetime of compassionate ministry." Obviously, it is not possible to fulfill Mr. Booth's desire; however, *World Missions* has been designed to impart a burden and vision for world evangelism. I was pleased to have Randy Adams as my neighboring missionary in Togo and also as a dear friend. He lives a life devoted to evangelism and establishing the indigenous church.

World Missions is designed primarily for use in overseas training programs. It will also be a blessing to students in North American Bible colleges, missionaries, national leaders, and all who are involved in world evangelism.

The Reverend N. A. Urshan, former long-time general superintendent of the United Pentecostal Church International, asserted that world evangelization requires, "The Whole Gospel to the Whole World by the Whole Church." The command of the Great Commission is to all Christians and not just a select few in the North American church. Many times in the past, missionaries have come from the Western world. This is quickly changing as the center of Christian gravity moves to other areas of the world. Missionaries are being sent out today from all over the world. This textbook addresses missionary topics that are relevant to all of these missionaries. It also gives a clear understanding of the indigenous church, priorities in world evangelism, and setup of Global Missions, United Pentecostal Church International. For those who will never be missionaries, it provides an understanding of the task, the missionary, and the objectives of the missionary cause.

James G. Poitras
Director of Education/Associates in Missions
Global Missions
United Pentecostal Church International

Lesson 1

What Is Missions?

Key Verse

"And they went forth, and preached every where, the Lord working with them, and confirming the word with signs following. Amen" (Mark 16:20).

Missions is going forth

Lesson Goal

To define and introduce missions

WHAT I HAVE LEARNED

To establish a biblical example that will help us understand what missions is, we will begin with the key verse of this lesson, Mark 16:20:

"And they went forth, and preached every where, the Lord working with them, and confirming the word with signs following. Amen."

After receiving the Great Commission (which will be studied in the next lesson), and the baptism of the Holy Ghost (Acts 2), the disciples went forth "every where." The Lord commanded them to preach and teach all men, and He worked "with them" confirming the word with signs following.

I.   MISSIONS INVOLVES "GOING FORTH."

They "<u>went forth.</u>" Philip went down to the city of Samaria (Acts 8:5) and later went unto Gaza, which is desert. Peter went to Caesarea to the house of Cornelius. Paul and Barnabas went out from Antioch to Cyprus, Pamphylia, Pisidia, Lycaonia, Lycia, and so on.

Jesus said, "<u>Go ye.</u>" The word *go* is inseparable to missions. Just as surely as there is a mission, there must be "going" to see it accomplished. "Going" is a vital part of the responsibility of the church. But to state that missions is only about going falls far short of the mark.

II.   MISSIONS INVOLVES BEING "SENT FORTH."

"Then he called his twelve disciples together, and gave them power and authority over all devils, and to cure diseases. And he sent them to preach the kingdom of God, and to heal the sick" (Luke 9:1-2).

This word *sent* is used quite frequently throughout the New Testament in the same sense that it is used here. It means to "set apart," i.e., to send out (properly, on a mission), literally or figuratively.

A. We know that Jesus Christ, as the Son of God, was sent into this world on a mission (John 3:16).

B. In Luke 10:1 we see that Jesus sent seventy more disciples (two by two), into every city and place that He was going to visit, saying, "The harvest truly is great, but the labourers are few: pray ye therefore the Lord of the harvest, that he would send forth labourers into his harvest." It is important to take note that the prayer request of Jesus was to pray that laborers would be "sent forth."

C. In Acts 13:1-4, the Bible relates that Barnabas and Saul (Paul) were set apart and "sent forth" by the church (verse 3) as well as by the Holy Ghost (verse 4). It is worthy to note that the church plays an important role in the sending forth of missionaries that God has called and set apart for this work. If the church will do her part in sending out men and women called of God, the Lord will do His part by equipping them, going with them, and working through them to accomplish His will and purpose.

Paul's closing remark to the Jews in Acts 28:28 states that "the salvation of God is sent unto the Gentiles, and that they will hear it." This "unto the Gentiles" means unto all nations of the world, i.e., every kindred, tongue, people, and nation. In Revelation 5:9 and 7:9, it is evident that this prophesy is fulfilled by those who are being sent forth on a mission by the Lord.

III.   MISSIONS INVOLVES "DOING."

To go and to be sent are essential but would be wasted effort without "doing" what one has been sent to do. The birth of Christ would have accomplished the going and sending aspect of the mission. However, the accomplishment of the mission required the living of a sinless life, the suffering and dying of the innocent for the guilty, the burial and glorious resurrection, and finally the ascension back to Heaven. That is the "doing" aspect.

The birth of a missions burden is essential. However, this birthing must go beyond the cradle of our mind and penetrate to the very fibers of our purpose in order to see the mission accomplished. There must be a "doing" of it.

Before his death, King David gave unto his son Solomon the plans for building the Temple and concluded by saying, "Be strong and of good courage, and do it" (I Chronicles 28:20).

By all means, we should think about it, talk about it, pray about it, preach, and even teach about it. Then at all costs, we must go, and our going must be accompanied with a sending by the Lord.

Nevertheless, all of these efforts are in vain if after arriving on the field we fail to set in motion the actual work of missions. Missions involves work!

"Just do it!"

IV.   MISSIONS IS "REACHING."

If we go forth, sent by the Lord, preaching and teaching as we are commanded, the result will be the reaching of a lost world. A good formula to remember is:

Preaching + Teaching = Reaching

In Luke 19:10 Jesus stated His mission, the very reason He came, and the reason for the Incarnation:

"For the Son of man is come to seek and to save that which was lost."

This verse well describes the mission of the church: seeking and saving of the lost. The mission of the church is nothing less than an extension of the ministry and mission of Jesus Christ. Jesus had a world mission in mind: "all nations; all the world; every creature." The world was always in His thoughts. "For God so loved the world, that He gave His only begotten Son." Why? "That the world through Him might be saved" (John 3:16-17).

One of Paul's favorite comparisons of the church was to the body of Christ. This is a powerful revelation. Consider the following carefully:

His hands, His feet, His eyes, His ears, and His mouth = **His body**.

Often when we think in these terms, we think of the miracles. However, while it is true that He changed water into wine, that was not His mission. He healed all manner of disease, opened blind eyes, raised the dead, and even walked on the water. But these supernatural acts were not the principal focus of His coming. He came to seek and to save lost humanity. This is the mission of the church.

> Missions states the reason for the existence of the church.

It must be remembered that missions is not primarily a process by which a society or culture is improved. It is a process by which lives are transformed and saved. Simply put, missions states the reason for the existence of the church. Someone said, "Missions is to the church what wood is to the fire."

In his book *Key to the Missionary Problem*, Andrew Murray reached the following conclusion concerning the importance of missions to the church:

Missions are the chief end of the church. The chief end of the ministry is to guide the church in this work, and to equip her for it. The chief end of the preaching to a congregation ought to be to train it to help to fulfill her destiny. And the chief end of every minister in this connection ought to be to fit himself thoroughly for this work. (Andrew Murray, *Key To The Missionary Problem*. Fort Washington, PA: CLC Publications, 1981.)

> "Where no wood is, there the fire goeth out" (Proverbs 26:20).

If, in fact, missions is to the church what wood is to the fire, then we must continue to add fuel to the flame. If we are going to see this world, for which Christ died, consumed by the flames of apostolic revival, the bosom of the church must have a continual burning. God's instruction to Moses concerning the fire upon the altar was that "it shall never go out" (Leviticus 6:13). The halls of history hold the memories of religious organizations, which in their early years burned with a zeal for missions but allowed that fire to go out.

> We must *go*! We must *send*! We must *do* it!
> We must *reach* the world! That is why the Savior died.

Some questions that must be answered to define missions include the following: (Answer in the space provided.)

1. What was the purpose of the birth of Jesus Christ (Matthew 1:23-26)?

    _____

2. What was the purpose of His ministry (Isaiah 61:1-4; Luke 4:16-20)?

    _____

3. What was the purpose of His suffering and death (Isaiah 53)?

    _____

4. What was the purpose of His burial and resurrection (Romans 6)?

    _____

5. What is the purpose of the church in the earth (Matthew 16:18-19)?

    _____

Jesus summed it all up in His final words before His ascension:

"Go ye therefore, and teach all nations, baptizing them in the name of the Father, and of the Son, and of the Holy Ghost: teaching them to observe all things whatsoever I have commanded you: and, lo, I am with you alway, even unto the end of the world. Amen" (Matthew 28:19-20).

"And he said unto them, Go ye into all the world, and preach the gospel to every creature. He that believeth and is baptized shall be saved; but he that believeth not shall be damned" (Mark 16:15-16).

WHAT HAVE YOU LEARNED?

Give short answers to the following questions.

1. What were the results of the preaching of the disciples as they went forth?

_____

_____

_____

2. What does the word *sent* most often mean in the New Testament?

_____

_____

_____

3. Describe the role of the church in sending out missionaries.

_____

_____

_____

4. What did David tell Solomon after giving him the plans for the building of the Temple? _____

_____

_____

5. Give one Bible verse that describes the mission of Jesus Christ.

_____

_____

6. What is the reason for the existence of the church?

_____

_____

_____

7. What do we learn about the mission of Jesus Christ by studying Isaiah 53?

_____

_____

_____

8. Why is the revelation of the church as the body of Christ powerful?

_____

_____

_____

9. Throughout history, what has been the fate of religious organizations that lost their zeal for missions? _____

_____

_____

10. Name four actions that well describe the work of missions.
    A. _____
    B. _____
    C. _____
    D. _____

Personal Study Notes

Lesson 2

What Is the Great (together) Commission?

Key Verse

"But ye shall receive power, after that the Holy Ghost is come upon you: and ye shall be witnesses unto me both in Jerusalem, and in all Judaea, and in Samaria, and unto the uttermost part of the earth" (Acts 1:8).

Lesson Goal

To define and provide understanding of the Great Commission

WHAT I HAVE LEARNED

The Great Commission is a simple declaration that has the potential to affect the entire world when put into practice.

Because of the importance of the Great Commission, it is needful that we carefully consider this subject. Jesus repeated or spoke of the Great Commission at least three times during the forty days between His resurrection and His ascension. The fact of this being reported by all four of the Gospels reveals its importance.

Jesus spoke of the Great Commission on the following three occasions:

1. While at the table in Jerusalem (Mark 16:14-18; John 20:22-23)
2. On a mountain in Galilee (Matthew 28:18-20).
3. On the Mount of Olives just before His ascension (Luke 24:45-51; Acts 1:6-9).

The Great Commission is not simply a
suggestion or request but rather a commandment.

The Great Commission is not simply a suggestion or request but rather a commandment. Peter made direct reference to this fact at the house of Cornelius in Acts 10:42 saying, "And he [Jesus] commanded us to preach unto the people."

The Great Commission is the basis of the authority of the church. This Great Commission is not a commandment addressed only to the apostles but is an irrevocable order addressed to the church. When a person receives a commission to do something, he also receives the authority to act on the behalf of the one giving the commission. The apostle Paul recognized this when he said, "We are ambassadors for Christ" (II Corinthians 5:20). The Lord has given the commission with the authority to accomplish the task.

With authority comes power. Jesus told His disciples, "Tarry ye in the city of Jerusalem, until ye be endued with power from on high" (Luke 24:49). He followed up by saying, "But ye shall receive power, after that the Holy Ghost is come upon you" (Acts 1:8). So we see that God gave an order with the promise of power to carry it out. The Great Commission constitutes the *marching orders* of the New Testament church. Therefore, when an individual, called of God and filled with the Holy Ghost, goes forth to preach or teach the gospel of Jesus Christ, this is in direct obedience to the Great Commission. This is why the apostle Paul could say, "For I am not ashamed of the gospel of Christ: for it is the power of God unto salvation to every one that believeth; to the Jew first, and also to the Greek" (Romans 1:16).

Authority with power brings responsibility. If authority brings power, then it also carries with it responsibility. The greater the authority is, the greater the responsibility is. Certainly the people who are entrusted with greater degrees of authority are the ones who also carry greater responsibilities. No person has any greater responsibility than the one who has been called of God and endued with heavenly authority and power to go forth preaching and teaching the eternal Word of God. This individual carries the responsibility of communicating the saving gospel of Jesus Christ to eternal souls that are lost.

The responsibility to accomplishing the Great Commission rests on every member of the church.

> The church of Jesus Christ has a two-fold responsibility:
> (1) To the Lord
> (2) To a lost world for whom Christ died.

I.   IT IS CALLED THE *GREAT* COMMISSION.

It is great for many reasons:

- Its Giver is the greatest of all.
- His motivation was "His great love" (Ephesians 2:4).
- The greatest price was paid to insure its effectiveness—the blood of the Lamb of God (I Peter 1:18-19).
- Its vehicle is "great grace" (Acts 4:33; Titus 2:11).
- Its goal is the greatest. It concerns "all the world; every creature; all flesh" (Matthew 28:19; Mark 16:15).
- Its results are the greatest—complete salvation for the eternal soul (Romans 1:16).

II.   IT IS THE GREAT *CO-MISSION.*

Co-mission means, of course, we are not going or doing alone. Notice that Jesus said, "Lo, I am with you alway, even unto the end of the world" (Matthew 28:20). Mark 16:20 states, "They went forth, and preached every where, the Lord working with them, and confirming the word with signs following." This is why we can go and we can accomplish the mission set before us.

> He that goes with us and does through us
> is greater than the task that is set before us.

We will now look at the following accounts of the Great Commission, including Acts 1:8 because of its importance to the mission of the church: Matthew 28:16–20; Mark 16:14–20; Luke 24:44-53; John 20:19-23; Acts 1:8.

A.   Matthew 28:19-20

"Go ye therefore, and teach all nations, baptizing them in the name of the Father, and of the Son, and of the Holy Ghost: teaching them to observe all things whatsoever I have commanded you: and, lo, I am with you alway, even unto the end of the world. Amen."

In our brief study of each of the five accounts of the Great Commission, we will pay close attention to the action words or verbs that are addressed to the church. In these verses of Matthew 28, we see the verbs *go, teach, baptize,* and *observe* used. Now let us consider the implication of these verbs.

1. Who is to go, teach, and baptize? You.
2. To whom are you to go? All nations.
3. What do you teach them? To obey all of the commandments that Jesus taught.
4. What is His promise for you? "I am with you always, even unto the end of the world."

B.   Mark 16:15-20

"And he said unto them, Go ye into all the world, and preach the gospel to every creature. He that believeth and is baptized shall be saved; but he that believeth not shall be damned. And these signs shall follow them that believe; In my name . . . And they went forth, and preached every where, the Lord working with them, and confirming the word with signs following. Amen."

Notice *go, preach, believe,* and *baptize* are associated with the term *saved.*

- If you go in faith, preaching the gospel and baptizing those who believe, this will work towards the salvation of their souls. Included is the promise of signs and miracles to those who believe.
- This is a manifestation of the promised presence and power of Jesus Christ.

The Gospel of Mark closes by saying that the disciples, in fact, went forth and preached everywhere and the Lord worked with them and confirmed His word with signs following. They went; we must go. They preached everywhere; we must preach everywhere. The Lord worked with them; He will work with us! Amen.

C.   Luke 24:45-49

"Then opened he their understanding, that they might understand the scriptures, and said unto them, Thus it is written, and thus it behoved Christ to suffer, and to rise from the dead the third day: and that repentance and remission of sins should be preached in his name among all nations, beginning at Jerusalem. And ye are witnesses of these things. And, behold, I send the promise of my Father upon you: but tarry ye in the city of Jerusalem, until ye be endued with power from on high."

Luke tells us that Jesus did something special for these disciples: He "opened their understanding that they might understand the scriptures." It is important to take note that the apostles had a clear understanding of what they were to do.

After opening their understanding, Jesus gave them the message they were to preach: "Repentance and remission of sins in His name among all nations, beginning at Jerusalem."

After instructing them as to what they should preach, Jesus reminded them of the promise of the Father, which is the Holy Ghost, and that they must tarry in Jerusalem until they had received this promise that would endue them with heavenly power.

> To be truly effective as a preacher of the gospel,
> you must be filled with the Holy Ghost.

D.   John 20:20-23

"And when he had so said, he shewed unto them his hands and his side. Then were the disciples glad, when they saw the Lord. Then said Jesus to them again, Peace be unto you: as my Father hath sent me, even so send I you. And when he had said this, he breathed on them, and saith unto them, Receive ye the Holy Ghost: whose soever sins ye remit, they are remitted unto them; and whose soever sins ye retain, they are retained."

Here Jesus talked of sending His disciples out. This is the commissioning of these men, and once again, He told them that they should receive the Holy Ghost.

Some would teach that at this point the disciples actually received the Holy Ghost, but the Bible does not support this teaching. They did not actually receive the Holy Ghost until the Day of Pentecost. (See Acts 2:1-4.)

Verse 32 mentions the remission of sins again. Paul said, "In the mouth of two or three witnesses shall every word be established" (II Corinthians 13:1).

E.   Acts 1:8

"But ye shall receive power, after that the Holy Ghost is come upon you: and ye shall be witnesses unto me both in Jerusalem, and in all Judaea, and in Samaria, and unto the uttermost part of the earth."

This verse has been rightly called "The Pentecostal Commission" because of the reference to the infilling of the Holy Ghost. The Pentecostal Commission can only be carried out by a Pentecostal church with Pentecostal power.

Acts 1:8 is not difficult to understand. The power to be a witness unto Jesus comes only after one receives the Holy Ghost. Notice the order given for the spreading of the gospel is exactly according to the order followed by the church in the Book of Acts: (1) Jerusalem, (2) Judaea, (3) Samaria, (4) the uttermost part of the earth.

Notice this last part, "the uttermost part of the earth," is the only part yet to be completely fulfilled. The responsibility to see this accomplished is upon you and me.

> We must *go*, we must *preach*, we must *teach*, and in doing so, we will *reach* this world with the saving message of Jesus Christ.

In summary, the Great Commission is a direct order to the church to go by faith into every nation of the world, teaching and preaching the gospel of Jesus Christ. This includes the necessity of repentance, baptism in Jesus' name for the remission of sins, and also the promise of the Holy Ghost. One needs to understand that those who believe and obey will be saved. When this is done, expect that the Lord will manifest His presence and power by confirming the Word with signs following.

Rick Warren, in his book *The Purpose Driven Church*, says, "A great commitment to the Great Commandment and the Great Commission will produce a great church." (Rick Warren, *The Purpose Driven Church*. Grand Rapids: Zondervan Publishing House, 1995, 102.)

WHAT HAVE YOU LEARNED?

Give short answers to the following questions.

1. Name the three occasions on which Jesus spoke of the Great Commission.
   A. _____
   B. _____
   C. _____

2. To whom is the Great Commission addressed?
   _____
   _____

3. Identify the power promised to the disciples.
   _____
   _____
   _____

4. Who is responsible for the fulfillment of the Great Commission?
   _____
   _____

5. Why is it called the *Great* Commission?
   _____
   _____
   _____

6. What is meant by "Co-mission"?
   _____
   _____
   _____

7. Give at least five action words (verbs) directly associated with the Great Commission.

   A. _____

   B. _____

   C. _____

   D. _____

   E. _____

8. List the five accounts of the Great Commission studied in this lesson.

   A. _____

   B. _____

   C. _____

   D. _____

   E. _____

9. Write out in full the *"Pentecostal Commission."*

   _____

   _____

   _____

   _____

10. Write a paragraph describing the contents of the Great Commission.

   _____

   _____

   _____

   _____

   _____

   _____

   _____

   _____

   _____

   _____

   _____

   _____

   _____

   _____

Lesson 3

Mission Impossible?

Key Verse

"Say not ye, There are yet four months, and then cometh harvest? behold, I say unto you, Lift up your eyes, and look on the fields; for they are white already to harvest" (John 4:35).

Lesson Goal

To reflect upon world and region population statistics and our mission

WHAT I HAVE LEARNED

The title of this lesson refers to a question that has often surfaced in the minds of sincere Christians and religious organizations throughout the centuries of the existence of the church: Is it possible to reach the entire population of the world with the gospel of Jesus Christ? After all, the church has been in existence now for almost two thousand years. The population of the world has exploded well beyond seven billion during this generation. Every twelve years the world's population increases by another one billion people. Factoring in the mortality rate, 237,211 people are added to our planet each day ("2014 World Population Data Sheet," Population Reference Bureau, Washington, DC, 2014). Is reaching the world with the gospel an impossible mission?

I.   FACTS AND FIGURES ABOUT WORLD POPULATION

The Population Reference Bureau, an accepted authority on population levels and trends based in Washington, DC, estimates that the world population surpassed 7.238 billion in mid-2014. Of this total, 1.240 billion people live in the developed nations of the world, and 5.989 billion people live in the less-developed countries. Based on the structure of the Global Missions regions and information from PRB, Africa Region had a mid-2014 population of 959 million; Asia Region, 3,639.6 million; Central America/Caribbean Region, 209.6 million; Europe/Middle East Region, 1,240 million; Pacific Region, 427.4 million; and South America Region, 408.4.

According to the PRB, the world's population increases annually by more than eighty-six million people. One hundred sixty-two of the 165 people added to the world's population every minute live in the less-developed countries. The PRB estimates the mid-2030 population will reach 8.444 million and soar to 9.683 million in mid-2050.[1]

Some estimate that 2.168 billion people in the world adhere to some form of Christianity.[2] According to the nondenominational World Christian Database, a project of the Center for the Study of Global Christianity at Gordon-Conwell Theological Seminary, Christianity has a growth rate of 1.38 percent. However, Islam's growth rate is 1.84 percent; Bahai Faith's, 1.70 percent; Sikhism's, 1.62 percent; Jainism's, 1.57 percent; and Hinduism's, 1.52 percent.[3] Even with this the followers of Jesus Christ are growing more rapidly than at any time in history, especially in Africa, Latin America, and parts of Asia. However, please note that this surge of Christianity has not kept pace with the world's population explosion.

> *Teacher's Note:*
> *Research your own regional and national population statistics and insert them here.*

Are we to accept the idea that our God has commissioned us to an impossible task? Are we to be content with the statistics that tell us that the false and idolatrous teachings of world religions are going to brush the face of this earth like a giant broom, sweeping untold millions into a hopeless, eternal lake of fire?

---

[1] *http://www.prb.org/pdf14/2014-world-population-data-sheet_eng.pdf*, accessed December 4, 2014.
[2] .*http://www.globalreligiousfutures.org/explorer/custom#/?subtopic=15&chartType=pie&data_type =number&year=2010&religious_affiliation=all&countries=Worldwide&age_group=all&pdfMode =false*, accessed December 4, 2014.
[3] *http://www.foreignpolicy.com/articles/2007/05/13/the_list_the_worlds_fastest_growing_religions*, accessed December 4, 2014.

Jesus said, "Say not ye, There are yet four months, and then cometh harvest? behold, I say unto you, Lift up your eyes, and look on the fields; for they are white already to harvest" (John 4:35).

An interesting calculation was made some years ago that is worthy of mention here. If only one Christian was on the face of the earth, and he determined to reach one other person within a year, and they determined to reach one other person each for the following year and this process continued, in only thirty-three years there would be over four billion Christians. If this process were projected for thirty-four years, there would be 8,589,934,592 Christians. From time to time we have taught this same concept of "each one reach one" in our churches.

Consider that a city of over half a million could be reached in twenty years, a nation of eight million could be reached in twenty-four years, a nation of over sixteen million in twenty-five years; a nation of over thirty-two million in twenty-six years, sixty-four million in twenty-seven years, and so forth. Mission Impossible?

II.   GROWTH OF THE EARLY CHURCH

Follow the progress reports of the first-century church taken from the Book of Acts:

- Acts 2:1-4 - Pentecost, the beginning - 120 received the Holy Ghost.
- Acts 2:37-41 - That same day 3,000 were baptized and added unto the church. (3120 members)
- Acts 4:4 - About 5,000 men were converted. (This doesn't even include the women and children.)
- Acts 5:14 - Multitudes (plural) both men and women. (No total given, just multitudes)
- Acts 6:7 - The number of disciples multiplied greatly and a great number of priests were converted.
- Acts 9:31 - The churches were multiplied. (Meaning the number of churches increased)
- Acts 11:24 - Much people was added unto the Lord.
- Acts 16:5 - The churches increased in number daily.

As the disciples of the first-century church went forth preaching and teaching the gospel of Jesus Christ, the results were astounding. It has been said, "Any fool can count the seeds in one apple, but only God can count the apples in one seed." In the parables of Jesus, the seed was the Word of God and the field was the world.

Consider the following account of Paul's activities at Ephesus from Acts 19:

"But when divers were hardened, and believed not, but spake evil of that way before the multitude, he departed from them, and separated the disciples, disputing daily in the school of one Tyrannus. And this continued by the space of two years; so that all they which dwelt in Asia heard the word of the Lord Jesus, both Jews and Greeks" (Acts 19:9-10).

They disputed daily.

Notice the frequent use of the word *daily* in the history of the early church:

- Acts 2:46 - They continuing *daily* with one accord . . . (This speaks of the daily actions of the church)
- Acts 2:47 - The Lord added to the church *daily* . . . (The Lord added daily because they continued daily)
- Acts 3:2 - There were *daily* prayer meetings at the Temple.
- Acts 5:42 - *Daily* in the Temple and in every house, they ceased not to teach and preach Jesus Christ.
- Acts 6:1 - There was a *daily* ministration of the word of God.
- Acts 16:5 - The churches were established in the faith and increased in number *daily*.
- Acts 17:11 - They searched the Scriptures *daily*.
- Acts 17:17 - *Daily* y discussions were held in the synagogues as well as in the marketplaces.
- Acts 19:9 - *Daily* discussions were held in the school of Tyrannus.

The daily activities of the New Testament church were the key to their success in evangelizing their generation.

> Daily, daily, daily, they ceased not!

And as long as they did their daily things, the Lord did His daily things. He added to the church daily. This last mention of the word *daily* in Acts 19:9 is of particular interest. During a two year period, "all they which dwelt in Asia" heard the word of God, whether Jews or Greeks.

"All they which dwelt in Asia heard the word."

What an interesting statement! This in itself gives hope of reaching the entire world with the gospel. If we believe the same things, preach and teach the same things, and put into practice the same principles, surely we will see the same results.

Someone said that if all unsaved people in the world were to line up single file at your front door, the line would reach around the world thirty times. This line would grow by thirty-two kilometers each day. If you were to drive a car at eighty kilometers per hour for ten hours a day, it would take you four years and forty days to get to the end of this line of lost souls. And by then it would have increased in length by 48,279 kilometers.

III. MISSION IMPOSSIBLE?

Perhaps if we attempt this task of world evangelism depending upon our own power and ability, we would quickly conclude that, yes, it is "Mission Impossible." But if we approach this task from a biblical standpoint, all the time leaning on the all-sufficient power of the Almighty, and go forth in faith and obedience, we will say in the end "Mission Accomplished."

To conclude this lesson, let us look into the inspired writings of the prophet Isaiah as he spoke concerning an abundant harvest of souls that would come:

> "Arise, shine; for thy light is come, and the glory of the LORD is risen upon thee. For, behold, the darkness shall cover the earth, and gross darkness the people: but the LORD shall arise upon thee, and his glory shall be seen upon thee. And the Gentiles shall come to thy light, and kings to the brightness of thy rising. Lift up thine eyes round about, and see: all they gather themselves together, they come to thee: thy sons shall come from far, and thy daughters shall be nursed at thy side. Then thou shalt see, and flow together, and

thine heart shall fear, and be enlarged; because the abundance of the sea shall be converted unto thee, the forces of the Gentiles shall come unto thee" (Isaiah 60:1-5).

Truly there is a great harvest in the field awaiting this New Testament church. May she arise to meet the challenge of this hour. Amen

WHAT HAVE YOU LEARNED?

Give short answers to the following questions.

1. According to the Population Reference Bureau's statistics, what was the population of the world in mid-2014?

   _____

2. What is the projected population of the world for the year 2050?

   _____

3. Write a paragraph and explain the concept of "each one reach one."

   _____
   _____
   _____
   _____
   _____
   _____
   _____
   _____
   _____
   _____
   _____
   _____
   _____
   _____

4. According to the Bible, how many people became converts in Acts 2?

   _____

5. What does the Bible say happened during the two-year period that Paul taught in the school of Tyrannus in Acts 19?

_____

_____

6. What seems to have been the key to success of the evangelism by the first-century church?

_____

_____

7. In your own words, explain the prophecy of Isaiah 61:1-5 as it pertains to the New Testament church.

_____

_____

_____

_____

_____

_____

_____

_____

_____

_____

Personal Study Notes

Lesson 4

Everyone Must Give or Go

Key Verse

"For unto whomsoever much is given, of him shall be much required: and to whom men have committed much, of him they will ask the more" (Luke 12:48).

Lesson Goal

To understand the responsibility of every member of the church to be involved in world missions

WHAT I HAVE LEARNED

I.   WE HAVE A RESPONSIBILITY.

With revelation of truth and blessing comes responsibility. What greater responsibility could anyone have than that of the church to reach a world of lost souls with the only saving message, that of the death, burial, and resurrection of Jesus Christ?

The children of Israel were recipients of the blessing of God to Abraham. They were also enlightened by the revelation of the one, true and living God, Creator of Heaven and earth. This placed a great responsibility upon their shoulders to act as a conductor of this blessing and revelation to the Gentile world around them. They were to be a light in the world of darkness, for God had said unto Abraham, "In thee shall all families of the earth be blessed" (Genesis 12:3).

In the same sense, the church has the greatest responsibility of all, communicating the saving gospel of Jesus Christ to a lost world. Jesus said, "For unto whomsoever much is given, of him shall be much required: and to whom men have committed much, of him they will ask the more" (Luke 12:48).

Surely those whose sins have been forgiven and washed away and who have been filled with the Holy Spirit are blessed above all men and women. These privileged people who have received the revelation of God in Christ reconciling the world unto Himself are greatly blessed. However, to whom much is given, much is required. We have a responsibility!

This responsibility is not just to the pastors, deacons, or other leaders of the church. It is to every member of the body of Christ.

II.   EVERYONE MUST GIVE OR GO.

It has been said: "Some give by going and others go by giving." This simply means that everyone must be involved in the process of sending or taking the gospel of Jesus Christ to every nation, people, kindred, and tongue in the earth.

> Some give by going and others go by giving.

Some will give but will never go because they lack the call; others will give by their going because they are called.

One of the first questions on the application for Global Missions appointment with the UPCI is concerning the candidate's personal history of giving to support the work of Global Missions. The wise men that make up the Global Missions Board have learned that if people have a genuine call and burden, they will express it by giving personally to the cause of world missions.

Not everyone can go; but everyone can give. However, giving is not limited to finances. One can give oneself in prayer and fasting for the harvest. One can also give his or her talents and abilities.

The following story was found in a local newspaper several years ago: The small child attending a Christian school in Africa, who gave his teacher a beautiful shell as a Christmas present, knew the real secret of life. When the teacher learned he had walked many miles to find the extraordinary shell, she said to the footsore boy, "You should not have gone all that way to get a gift for me." His eyes brightened as he answered, "The long walk is part of the gift."

There is no real giving without the giving of yourself.

III.   GIVE AND IT SHALL BE GIVEN UNTO YOU.

In a later lesson we will take a careful look at the church at Antioch where the disciples were first called Christians. (See Acts 11:26.) However, for this lesson we will only mention that the church at Antioch was missions minded. It was the church from which Paul based all of his missionary journeys. Why? Obviously the church at Antioch was a giving church.

Not everyone at Antioch went to the mission field, but it seems reasonable that those who did not go, gave to help send men like Paul and Barnabas who were definitely called of God (Acts 13:1-4).

When the local church involves itself in giving to send missionaries to a foreign land, that missionary becomes an extension of the ministry of that local assembly. The members will be able to rejoice with great joy as reports of the harvest come in from the field because they are involved with the fulfillment of the Great Commission of the Lord. They will have played a vital part in the harvest of souls and will feel more of a sense of responsibility to the rest of the world. Their prayer time will be more meaningful as they visit these foreign lands on their knees in prayer before the throne of God. Not only will their burden become greater for the foreign fields, but their burden will increase for the local community as well.

IV.   AND THEY GAVE.

In II Corinthians 8:1-5, we read of the generosity of the churches of Macedonia. They first gave themselves to the Lord and then gave sacrificially (Paul said "beyond their power") to the work of God abroad.

When the local church puts "Global Missions" at the top of its priorities, it is putting the kingdom of God in first place. Jesus said, "But seek ye first the kingdom of God, and his righteousness; and all these things shall be added unto you" (Matthew 6:33).

God will bless the local assembly because it has set its eyes on the fields that are white already to harvest.

Every local church should have a "Global Missions" program and receive an offering designated to this cause on a regular basis, preferably once every month. This is regardless of where this church is located in the world. The pastor should encourage the people to give liberally and then lead them in giving.

> Giving to world missions is the will of God for every local assembly.

Not only will God bless the finances of the church, but He will also send spiritual blessings that cannot be measured. Churches who have faithfully involved themselves with giving to missions through the years have a history of being churches with a passion for souls at home and abroad. The fire of revival seems to always burn there.

Perhaps one of the great sins of the modern church is that of selfishness. God never intended for the church to turn His blessings inwardly upon itself. Rather, He set the example that the church should follow, that being to turn His blessings outwardly unto the lost souls for which Christ died.

V.   GO YE INTO ALL THE WORLD

The first commandment given from the Lord unto Paul (while on the road to Damascus) was, "Arise, and go into the city, and it shall be told thee what thou must do" (Acts 9:6).

The ministry of the great apostle to the Gentiles began with the commandment "go," and throughout his life this seemed to be a never-ending quest. Paul became the writer of over two-thirds of the books of the New Testament, founder of a majority of the churches mentioned in the New Testament, successful missionary, pastor, evangelist, teacher, and soulwinner. A Christian. What an inspiration for every preacher of the gospel!

Why did Paul go, and go, and keep on going? Was it because of a driving desire to travel and see the world? Hardly. Perhaps it was his ambition to rise to great heights among his fellow ministers. Never! It was, however, because of a sure calling. He had heard that certain sound, that of the voice of the Lord. He could never forget it and unlike Jonah of old, he would not run from that voice and calling. It was this same Paul who said, "For the gifts and calling of God are without repentance" (Romans 11:29) and yet again, "Yea, woe is unto me, if I preach not the gospel!" (I Corinthians 9:16).

> The call of God is of utmost importance.

A young, aspiring preacher was contemplating what he felt to be the will of God for his ministry. He felt that God was calling him to plant a church in a town where there was no Apostolic (Pentecostal) church. Therefore, he decided it wise to ask counsel from an older, wiser pastor who had already traveled that same path successfully. The older pastor gave this counsel:

> If you are 100 percent sure that God has called you to that city, then go with your mind made up that you are going to stay. Settle the matter within yourself from the start: I'm here in the will of God and I'm going to stay according to the will of God. When difficulties and problems come—and they will—you will be able to stand firm because you know that you are there according to the will of God and problems cannot drive you away. Even if Satan himself comes against you, the matter has already been settled: I'm staying because it is the will of God! But if you are not convinced within yourself that it is God's will, you will question yourself every time problems arise and you will often consider quitting and leaving because of that uncertainty.

The calling must be received from God and not from someone else. Pastors cannot call someone into the ministry and neither can a missionary. Unfortunately this has happened at times and has always proven to be a costly mistake. God still gives a clear and precise call to men and places them into the ministry.

VI.   AND THEY WENT FORTH.

In Acts 13:1-4, we read the inspiring account of the sending of Barnabas and Paul from Antioch. At the first look, it seems these two men were celebrities of a sort in the church. What a privilege to be sent out on an expense-paid, two-year vacation! However, take a second look and consider the following Scriptures passages:

> "It seemed good unto us, being assembled with one accord, to send chosen men unto you with our beloved Barnabas and Paul, men that have hazarded their lives for the name of our Lord Jesus Christ" (Acts 15:25-26).

Some gave. Others went. Nevertheless, both were involved in accomplishing the Great Commission of the Lord Jesus Christ.

> "Wherefore seeing we also are compassed about with so great a cloud of witnesses, let us lay aside every weight, and the sin which doth so easily beset us, and let us run with patience the race that is set before us, looking unto Jesus the author and finisher of our faith; who for the joy that was set before him endured the cross, despising the shame, and is set down at the right hand of the throne of God" (Hebrews 12:1-2).

Amen.

WHAT HAVE YOU LEARNED?

Give short answers to the following questions.

1. What was the responsibility of Israel concerning the blessing of Abraham and the revelation of the true God? _____
   _____
   _____
   _____

2. What is the greatest responsibility of all? _____
   _____
   _____
   _____

3. Who must give to the cause of "Global Missions"?

_____

_____

_____

4. What are some of the blessings that a local church can expect from God because of its faithful giving to support "Global Missions"?

_____

_____

_____

5. Who should be the first to give to the cause of missions in the local church? Why? _____

_____

_____

_____

6. From where did Paul base his missionary journeys?

_____

_____

7. What one qualification is the most important for the person seeking to go into the field of "Global Missions"? Why?

_____

_____

_____

8. What happened to Paul (Saul) while on the road to Damascus that set the course for his life? _____

_____

_____

_____

9. Who accompanied Paul on his first missionary journey?

_____

_____

10. Describe the plan that the local church should have for the support of world missions. _____

_____

_____

_____

_____

_____

Lesson 5

What Is a Missionary?

Key Verse

"As they ministered to the Lord, and fasted, the Holy Ghost said, Separate me Barnabas and Saul for the work whereunto I have called them" (Acts 13:2).

Lesson Goal

To understand the calling and the work of a missionary

WHAT I HAVE LEARNED

Many wrong concepts are in the world about a missionary. Therefore, the first thing that will need to be established is what a missionary is not.

I.   WHAT A MISSIONARY IS NOT

A.   Not necessarily North American or European

Nationality does not determine the qualification of an individual called of God.

B.   Not a guaranteed source of foreign income

It is certain that they will help with needs according to their ability but this is not their reason for existence, and they should not be required to do so.

C. Not the "Papa" of the nationals

This leads to erroneous concepts. The missionaries are brothers and sisters in Christ. They are fellow laborers in the harvest.

D. Not perfect

They are on the same road to perfection as other Christians. They are human beings and can make mistakes just like everyone else.

E. Not God

Therefore, they cannot do all things, they do not know all things, and they cannot be in two places at the same time. They are limited in their abilities and possibilities.

II. WHAT A MISSIONARY IS

Let us now go to the Word of God to establish a biblical concept of a missionary. In order to do this, we will begin with Acts 13:1-4. Here we see that the Holy Ghost singled out Barnabas and Saul (Paul) to be sent forth to do a specific work. The church at Antioch responded quickly by sending them out on their first missionary journey.

> "Now there were in the church that was at Antioch certain prophets and teachers; as Barnabas, and Simeon that was called Niger, and Lucius of Cyrene, and Manaen, which had been brought up with Herod the tetrarch, and Saul. As they ministered to the Lord, and fasted, the Holy Ghost said, Separate me Barnabas and Saul for the work whereunto I have called them. And when they had fasted and prayed, and laid their hands on them, they sent them away. So they, being sent forth by the Holy Ghost, departed unto Seleucia; and from thence they sailed to Cyprus" (Acts 13:1-4).

A. Faithful to God and the church

This means they are born again of water and of the Spirit, faithful to God in obedience to His Word, maintaining a life of prayer and fasting, and proving themselves faithful and trustworthy in spiritual as well as material matters. They are sound in doctrine, faithful in paying tithes and in giving offerings, gaining and guarding the trust and confidence of fellow believers, and making their calling and election sure. Others will recognize these characteristics and acknowledge that they have a special calling and anointing for the work of missions.

B.   Called by God

All men and women are called to God for salvation but some receive a special call to a specific work. God singled out Moses when He spoke to him from the burning bush. Samuel received his call as a child while sleeping. Isaiah was worshiping in the Temple. Jeremiah was yet in his youth, and Ezekiel was among the captives of Judah in Babylon.

Acts 9:3-6 gives us the biblical account of the call of God to Saul of Tarsus, later named Paul. It was a definite call that came in an unforgettable way. This call would serve as both a reference point and an anchor throughout the life of the apostle Paul. He referred to the calling as:

a. "The high calling of God"   Philippians 3:14
b. "Holy calling"   II Timothy 1:9
c. "Heavenly calling"   Hebrews 3:1*

And finally, Paul stated, "The gifts and calling of God are without repentance" (Romans 11:29). Jesus said that many are called but few are chosen (Matthew 20:16). This statement could never be truer than in the area of missionary work. A missionary is someone who has been called and then chosen by God Himself.

C.   Has said yes to the Lord

Jesus said that many are called but few are chosen. Why would He call many yet only choose to use a few? The answer could be found in their willingness to say yes to the call.

God will use what has been made available to Him.

*This is assuming that Paul was the author of Hebrews.

After the widow of Zarephath made available to God her last handful of meal and last bit of oil, He multiplied it so that it outlasted the famine (I Kings 17:9-16). After the lad made available to Jesus his five barley loaves and two small fish, He took them and blessed them so the multitude could eat their fill and even have twelve basketsful remaining. Paul said, "If there be first a willing mind, it is accepted according to that a man hath, and not according to that he hath not" (II Corinthians 8:12).

Looking again at the positive response of Paul to the call of the Lord is inspiring here: "And he trembling and astonished said, Lord, what wilt thou have me to do?" (Acts 9:6).

A missionary has had his own "Damascus Road" experience and he too has asked, "What wilt thou have me to do?" He has made himself available.

D.   Someone who has been sent

Notice the use of the word *sent*:

* The church sent them (verse 3).
* The Holy Ghost sent them (verse 4).

The Holy Ghost spoke, the church obeyed by sending out Barnabas and Saul (Paul), and this was considered the action of the Holy Ghost. Do not underestimate the importance of the role of the church here. The church recognized their calling and laid their hands on them before sending them out. It could be said that the missionaries passed through the hands of the church before going to the field. This same process is followed in the United Pentecostal Church today.

The church, as the body of Christ, plays a vital role in the sending out of missionaries.

E.   Has a compassion for people

Matthew mentioned at least four times in his Gospel that Jesus had compassion toward others in need. He was moved with compassion when He saw the multitudes that were scattered as sheep having no shepherd. He was moved with compassion for the blind, the leper, the demon possessed, and the heartbroken. The parable of the Good Samaritan speaks of compassion for the hurting and troubled. Jesus concluded this parable in Luke 10:37 by saying, *"Go, and do thou likewise."* The parable of the Lost Sheep speaks of a compassion that compelled the shepherd to go out into the cold, dark night in search of that one lost lamb until he found it and brought it back to safety (Luke 15:1-7). Finally, the prodigal son who came home was welcomed by the warm arms of compassion (Luke 15:20).

Missionaries will carry a genuine love in their hearts for the people to whom they have been sent. They do not estimate their value by the color of their skin but by the price paid for their redemption, the blood of Christ. God will put this love in their hearts and help to maintain it. When frustrations and disappointments come, this love will continue to flow.

In the heart of every true missionary is a burning passion for lost souls. This is often referred to as a burden for souls. It is this burden coupled with their calling that causes them to leave behind the familiar surroundings of home and family to go to that sometimes-distant land, to share the good news of Jesus Christ.

F.   Acquainted with sacrifice

The name Barnabas means "Son of Consolation." This companion of Paul lived up to his name. He sold his land, brought the money, and laid it at the apostles' feet. He held back nothing; he gave his all to the work of God. Is it any wonder that the Lord mightily used Barnabas?

This story has often been repeated in the lives of men and women called of God to the work of missions. Jesus said, "If any man will come after me, let him deny himself, and take up his cross daily, and follow me" (Luke 9:23).

Charles H. Spurgeon, a well-known minister of the nineteenth century, once said:

> For Him I count as gain each loss,
> Disgrace for Him, renown;
> Well may I glory in His cross,
> While He prepares my crown!

G.   Must adjust to a different culture

This is always a challenge, and at times can be very difficult. Missionaries must learn a new language, customs, and traditions. They must adjust to the climate, changes in diet, formalities with the foreign government, and so forth. It requires patience and understanding from both the nationals and the missionaries. On the one hand, the missionaries have not been sent to change the culture of the nationals; but on the other hand, they cannot allow the different culture to undermine their personal convictions.

One must remember that the principles of the Word of God do not change with culture. God's Word is forever settled in Heaven. In the eyes of the Lord, there is only one church. It is not North American, European, Asian, or African. It is Christ-like. The principles of the Word of God apply to every culture on the face of the earth.

A fine line exists between tolerance and compromise. One must never compromise the truths of God's Word. Yet tolerance is a valuable quality. Paul said he was made a minister to the Gentiles "according to the gift of the grace of God" (Ephesians 3:7). Paul best stated how this gift operates in I Corinthians 9:19-23:

> "For though I be free from all men, yet have I made myself servant unto all, that I might gain the more. And unto the Jews I became as a Jew, that I might gain the Jews; to them that are under the law, as under the law, that I might gain them that are under the law; to them that are without law, as without law, (being not without law to God, but under the law to Christ,) that I might gain them that are without law. To the weak became I as weak, that I might gain the weak: I am made all things to all men, that I might by all means save some. And this I do for the gospel's sake, that I might be partaker thereof with you."

This does not speak of compromise but rather of an ability to adapt to different cultures and levels of society. Why? For the gospel's sake.

CONCLUSION

The work of missionaries speaks of the unfolding of the plan of God for making the gospel of Jesus Christ known to the entire world. This involves taking the gospel into areas where it has never been before. True missionaries will risk everything for the sake of the lost souls of this world. They see their mission as being more important than their own desires and goals. Their priorities are set with the accomplishment of their mission in mind. Their goal is to please and glorify God by delivering the whole world into His hands. It doesn't matter where they are stationed, for they are always at home in their Father's arms. They are soldiers of the Lord on the front line of the battle. Perhaps they are hidden from the eyes of many, but always within vision of He who sees all. They are men and women after God's own heart.

WHAT HAVE YOU LEARNED?

Give short answers to the following questions.

1. Name some of the wrong concepts about missionaries discussed in this lesson. _____
   _____
   _____
   _____

2. What is the role of the church in sending out missionaries?
   _____
   _____
   _____

3. Why is faithfulness in spiritual as well as material matters an important qualification of a missionary? _____
   _____
   _____

4. In what three ways did Paul refer to the call of God?
   A. _____
   B. _____
   C. _____

5. Why did Jesus say that many are called but few are chosen?

_____

_____

_____

6. Who was the "son of consolation" and why was he called this?

_____

_____

_____

7. What three things did Jesus require of those who would be His disciples?
   A. _____
   B. _____
   C. _____

8. List some problems a missionary might face in adjusting to a different culture. _____

_____

_____

_____

9. When is it permissible to change a principle of the Word of God in order to adapt to a culture? _____

_____

_____

_____

10. In your own words, describe what you think a missionary should be.

_____

_____

_____

_____

Lesson 6

What Are the Missionary's Objectives?

Key Verse

"And so were the churches established in the faith, and increased in number daily" (Acts 16:5).

Lesson Goal

To understand the biblical purpose, goals, and objectives of the missionary in the country where he or she labors

WHAT I HAVE LEARNED

Someone said, "If you aim at nothing, you are sure to hit nothing. But if you aim at the stars, you just might hit one." This teaches us that one must have a well-defined goal before there will be success. Every journey begins with one step. However, for that journey to end at the right destination, every following step must be in the right direction. For this reason, missionaries must have a clear concept of their own work as a missionary and of their proper relationship with the nationals.

Another person compared this to the scaffolding used in the erection of a building. The scaffolding is intended to be a temporary support for the building until it is completed. If the building collapses after the scaffolding is removed, what would your conclusion be?

If you were to ask several different Christian organizations "What are the objectives of your missionaries?" you would probably receive as many different answers. Some would say their purpose is to improve the overall living conditions of the people. Others would say to raise the level of education for the people or to build hospitals, schools, and/or clinics.

Although these are worthy objectives, they are by-products and are not at the heart of the purpose of missions. If this is not understood, chances are that strong institutions will be built but the church will remain weak.

I. WHAT IS THE BIBLICAL PURPOSE OF MISSIONS?

Jesus stated His purpose clearly in Matthew 16:18 when He said, "Upon this rock I will build my church." He came to seek and to save that which was lost (Luke 19:10) and to give His life as a ransom for many (Matthew 20:28). His death on the cross accomplished this ransom, and His glorious resurrection insured it. After giving the Great Commission to His disciples in His farewell address on the Mount of Olives, He ascended back up to His heavenly abode. After ten days, His Spirit gave birth to the church on the Day of Pentecost (Acts 2:1-4). This church would be the instrument by which He would accomplish His divine purpose of transmitting the saving gospel to all flesh.

Consider that the purpose of Jesus Christ was to establish His church and then the church would act as His body and as an extension of His ministry. Therefore, the primary goal of every missionary should be to establish a New Testament church, based upon the teachings and principles of the Word of God, in the country to which God has sent him.

Jesus said the wise man built his house upon the rock (Matthew 7:24), and He, being the all-wise God who created all things by His wisdom (Psalm 104:24), said, "Upon this rock I will build my church; and the gates of hell shall not prevail against it" (Matthew 16:18). The church must be founded upon the rock, which is the Word of God and the revelation of the divinity of Jesus Christ, if it is to prevail against the gates of hell and the forces of the devil.

In order to accomplish this primary goal, it is vital that the missionary have the following objectives:

A. Establish the New Testament church upon the foundation of the apostles' doctrine

"And they continued stedfastly in the apostles' doctrine" (Acts 2:42).

"Built upon the foundation of the apostles and prophets, Jesus Christ himself being the chief corner stone" (Ephesians 2:20).

1. Preach the apostolic doctrine—Acts 2:38

The Great Commission includes the command to preach and gives the message that should be preached: repentance, baptism in Jesus' name for the remission of sins, and the gift of the Holy Ghost (Matthew 28:19; Mark 16:15-16; Luke 24:47-49; John 20:22; Acts 1:8; 2:38).

2. Teach the apostolic doctrine

The Great Commission includes the command to teach. We read that the New Testament church *"ceased not to teach"* Jesus Christ (Acts 5:42). The word *doctrine* implies instruction or learning, both of which are the result of teaching. There is a great potential of revival through the teaching of sound doctrine. This is easily seen in the fact that after Paul taught for only two years in the school of Tyrannus (in Ephesus), all of Asia heard the Word of God (Acts 19:10).

3. Practice the apostolic doctrine

It has often been said that you should practice what you preach. It rather could be said, "Preach what you practice." This is vital to the success of the ministry of the New Testament church. A preacher must live the message before he can successfully preach it to others. New Testament preaching must be preceded by New Testament practicing in order to be effective.

B. Establish, as soon as possible, training programs to train the nationals

"And the things that thou hast heard of me among many witnesses, the same commit thou to faithful men, who shall be able to teach others also" (II Timothy 2:2).

1.   Bible schools

Bible schools play a vital role in the fulfillment of the Great Commission. A day school is preferable but night classes are often needed for those who work jobs and cannot attend day classes. Other options include a correspondence program and Portable Bible School (PBS). But for the training of future pastors and leaders, nothing is better than for them to spend two or three years in a well-organized Bible school that is staffed by God-called, Spirit-filled teachers. The training program should have as a goal to develop spiritual, soulwinning churches throughout the nation.

2.   Seminars

At times the missionary will want to plan a seminar for the leadership of the national church (pastors, evangelists, deacons, teachers, and so forth). This setting will give him the opportunity to address areas that need special attention or it can serve as a refresher course for the ministry. He may call in other missionaries, international guests, or delegate some of the more mature national pastors to help with the teaching. The training and equipping of the national leadership must be a top priority in order to see the New Testament church well established.

3.   On the job training

The classroom gives a wonderful opportunity for the missionary to teach, to train, and to influence the nationals. The many hours spent together are invaluable and help to build a strong and lasting relationship. However, nothing can take the place of hands-on-experience.

The airplane pilot learns much about the dynamics of flight in the classroom. But she does not learn to fly and control the airplane until she sits beside an experienced pilot, watching her movements, listening to her explanations and feeling the effects of her actions. Then and only then, is the aspiring pilot ready to take the controls into her hands and fly the airplane. This same principle is true with the ministry. Young or new ministers will benefit greatly by working closely with other, more mature ministers, who are wiser and more experienced.

C.   Establish a program of New Testament evangelism

"And daily in the temple, and in every house, they ceased not to teach and preach Jesus Christ" (Acts 5:42).

1.   Daily evangelism

The word *daily* is mentioned frequently in the Book of Acts. In Acts 2:46-47, something very interesting can be seen. Verse 46 says *they continued daily* and verse 47 says *the Lord added to the church daily* those that should be saved. They were busy with daily evangelism and the Lord was busy with daily additions to the church. The concept of the modern church seems to be more of a weekend-only evangelism but the missionary must encourage daily evangelism if he is to reach an entire nation.

> Daily evangelism is New Testament evangelism and it works!

2.   Personal evangelism

If *daily evangelism* is *New Testament evangelism*, then door-to-door, house-to-house, and one-on-one evangelism follows the model of the Book of Acts church. In Acts 2:46, we see that *daily* they were *from house to house*. Acts 5:42 says, "And daily in the temple, and in every house, they ceased not to teach and preach Jesus Christ."

- In Acts 20:20, Paul mentioned that while at Ephesus, he taught them "publickly and from house to house."
- The Holy Ghost sent Peter to the house of Cornelius, and God poured out His Spirit (Acts 10).
- After his miraculous release, Paul went to the house of the Philippian jailer where the jailer and his household were converted (Acts 16:25-34).
- After going to the house of one named Justus, Paul saw the conversion of many of the Corinthians, including Crispus, the chief ruler of the synagogue (Acts 18:7-8).
- After being shipwrecked on the island of Melita (Malta), Paul entered into the house where the father of the chief lay sick and healed him, and as a result many others were blessed by the ministry of Paul (Acts 28:7-8).

Nevertheless, we see that personal evangelism in the Book of Acts was not limited to the house. Philip was sent to the desert of Gaza on a venture of one-on-one, personal evangelism. There he met the Ethiopian eunuch and a miraculous conversion took place (Acts 8:26-40). In Acts 16:13-15, a prayer meeting was taking place on a riverbank and Lydia of Thyatira was converted.

Personal Evangelism works!

3. Mass evangelism

In recent years, the church has become acutely aware of the fulfillment of the prophecy of Joel 2:28—that in the last days, God would pour out of His Spirit upon all flesh. For example, in Ethiopia, literally tens of thousands have been filled with the Holy Ghost each year in mass evangelism crusades. So many reports have come in from around the world of several thousand receiving the Holy Ghost in one service that we are no longer amazed at such happenings.

Did this all start in the twentieth century? No. Let us look again to the Book of Acts, God's training manual for the church today. The first record of mass evangelism is found on the birthday of the church in Acts 2:38-41. Three thousand people gladly received the preaching of Peter and were baptized in Jesus' name, and we have reason to believe they also received the Holy Ghost. Acts 4:4 tells us that five thousand men believed and were converted. Acts 5:14 says multitudes were added to the Lord. That is mass evangelism.

Mass evangelism worked then and it works now!

D. Establish an Indigenous church

"And so were the churches established in the faith, and increased in number daily" (Acts 16:5).

Last but not least, the missionary must purpose from the beginning to establish an indigenous church in the country where he labors. Inasmuch as the next lesson will be a study of indigenous church principles of the New Testament church, we will not go into detail here. We will only try to define what is meant by *indigenous church*. The world is filled with many religious organizations. However, there is only one church, and it is the body of Christ. It lives because He lives, and it is powerful because His Spirit dwells within. Because of this, the New Testament church has the power to maintain itself and to expand itself. The indigenous church has three undeniable characteristics.

- **It is self-propagating,** which means it is expanding itself by the preaching of the gospel.

- **It is self-supporting,** meaning the necessary funds do not come from an outside source.

- **It is self-governing,** which means it produces and trains the needed leadership from among its own membership.

If we are amazed at the great accomplishments of the Book-of-Acts church, we should also be inspired to accomplish the same things today. Our God is the same, His Word has not changed, and we have received the same Spirit.

If we teach, preach, and practice the principles of the Book-of-Acts church, we will have the same results as the Book-of-Acts church.

In the pursuit of these objectives toward the establishment of the New Testament church, the man of God must be consecrated totally to the work of the Lord and maintain a life of effectual, fervent, daily prayer. Prayer is an indispensable element to the accomplishment of the mission. Amen.

WHAT HAVE YOU LEARNED?

Give short answers to the following questions.

1. Why must we have a well-defined goal to see success?

_____

_____

_____

2. What did Jesus state as being His purpose?

_____

_____

_____

3. Describe the biblical purpose of missions.

_____

_____

_____

4. What is meant by the term *apostolic doctrine*?

_____

_____

_____

_____

5. What are some benefits of attending a Bible school?

_____

_____

_____

_____

6. Why is *on the job training* important?

_____

_____

_____

7. Describe New Testament evangelism.

_____

_____

_____

_____

8. Give examples of personal evangelism in the Book of Acts.

_____

_____

_____

_____

9. Give examples of mass evangelism from the Book of Acts.

_____

_____

_____

_____

_____

10. Name and briefly explain the three characteristics of an indigenous church.

A. _____

_____

B. _____

_____

C. _____

_____

Personal Study Notes

Lesson 7

Indigenous Church Principles of the New Testament Church

Key Verse

"Upon this rock I will build my church; and the gates of hell shall not prevail against it" (Matthew 16:18).

Lesson Goal

To discover, define, and understand the principles upon which the New Testament church was established and to show how they are relevant to the church today

What I Have Learned

When you think of the New Testament church, what is the first thing that comes to mind? Without doubt, the answers would vary from one individual to another. A study of the New Testament reveals several analogies used in describing the church, such as the body of Christ (Ephesians 1:22-23), God's building (I Corinthians 3:9; Ephesians 2:21), a spiritual house (I Peter 2:5), and the bride of Christ (Revelation 21:2-9), to name a few.

By far, the most widely used analogy by Paul was that of the body of Christ. Thinking in terms of the church as the body of Christ, it is hard to imagine that the physical body of Jesus Christ could have been diseased, crippled, deformed, or weak. Can you picture in your mind, Jesus Christ hobbling around on crutches? Certainly not! The Bible says that after forty days of fasting in the wilderness, He came forth in the power of the Spirit.

In the same sense, it should be unimaginable that the New Testament church, which is the body of Jesus Christ in the earth, could be weak, crippled, or diseased. Yet when we look at some churches that have been established for many years, whether on the national or local level, we do not see the example of a strong, healthy body, functioning in the power of the Spirit. Rather, we see a church that is dependent upon foreign leadership, foreign money, and foreign evangelists. This is not according to the New Testament pattern we see in Acts. God never intended for His church to hobble through this world, trusting in these foreign crutches. Rather she should trust in Him with all of her heart, leaning not unto her own understanding.

Two things that must be kept in focus as you work to establish the indigenous church are:

1. **The importance of the local church.**
2. **Every member has a responsibility.**
   The local church is a living cell of the body of Christ working in unity, an expression of the body of Christ to its community, and the present manifestation of the kingdom of God with power. It is responsible for its mission and has the authority to see it accomplished.

The importance of the local church must never be underestimated. The strength of the local church determines the strength of the national church. It must be remembered that it is the growth, development, and maturity of local churches that will produce the need for a national organization. The natural result of strong, indigenous, local assemblies is a strong, indigenous, national work.

The New Testament church has the power to maintain itself and to expand itself. This is what is meant by the indigenous church. The indigenous church has three undeniable characteristics, which are *self-propagation*, *self-support*, and *self-government*. We will now look at each of these characteristics.

I. SELF-PROPAGATION

The church is God's agent to evangelize the world. This can be applied as well to a local church for the evangelization of a city or community. Though God has given some men and women a special gift and calling to be evangelists, every individual that has been filled with the Holy Ghost has received power to be a witness (Acts 1:8) and should be a soulwinner. The responsibility of evangelism rests upon the shoulders of every member of the body of Christ.

God designed the New Testament church to reproduce itself by means of preaching and teaching the gospel through the power of the Spirit. It has the potential of spreading itself to cover the face of the earth like a mighty flood of waters.

"But ye shall receive power, after that the Holy Ghost is come upon you: and ye shall be witnesses unto me both in Jerusalem, and in all Judaea, and in Samaria, and unto the uttermost part of the earth" (Acts 1:8).

Notice the progressive order given for the expansion of the church:

Jerusalem => Judaea => Samaria => Uttermost part of the earth.

Follow the fulfillment of this plan: Jerusalem (Acts 2-7); Judaea (Acts 8:1-4); Samaria (Acts 8:5-25); uttermost part of the earth (Acts 8:26—until now).

After her conversation with Jesus about the living water and the revelation of His identity, the Samaritan woman left her water pot and went to the people of her city as a witness of Jesus. As a result many believed on Jesus (John 4:1-42). After casting the unclean spirits out of the Gadarene possessed with a legion of devils (Mark 5:1-19), Jesus told him to go home to his friends and tell them of the great things the Lord had done for him (Mark 5:19). After his baptism and conversion, the Ethiopian eunuch returned to his country and likely testified of his experience to his own people (Acts 8:26-39). These all acted out of a sense of responsibility.

Who would better know how to reach a Samaritan than a Samaritan would? A Gadarene than a Gadarene? Or an Ethiopian than a fellow Ethiopian? Who could better witness to a European than a European? A Chinese than another Chinese? Or an African than a fellow African? God has so designed the gospel to be adaptable to every climate, race, and to every social and economic level on the earth. It fills the need of the European, Chinese, African, or American. Therefore, if the gospel seed is properly planted, it will produce an indigenous church in any village, town, city, or nation upon the face of the earth.

And that indigenous church will in turn reproduce itself after its kind over and over again.

> "And so were the churches established in the faith, and increased in number daily" (Acts 16:5).

Jesus said the kingdom of Heaven (the church) is like a grain of mustard seed, which a man sowed in his field. This seed (the Word of God) is "the least of all seeds: but when it is grown, it is the greatest among herbs, and becometh a tree" (Matthew 13:31-32).

The interpretation given by Daniel of Nebuchadnezzar's dream in Daniel 2 included a prophecy about the kingdom of God. Daniel said the stone that was cut out without hands, which smote the image upon his feet, became a great mountain and filled the whole earth (Daniel 2:31-35).

An interesting statement in Isaiah 60:22 pertains to the church: "A little one shall become a thousand, and a small one a strong nation."

The potential of the New Testament church in any generation is limited only by her silence: if she does not proclaim the gospel, remains stationary, and she does not go.

> "He that goeth forth and weepeth, bearing precious seed, shall doubtless come again with rejoicing, bringing his sheaves with him" (Psalm 126:6).

II.   SELF-GOVERNMENT

Self-government is vital to the day-by-day operation of the church. This goal should be kept in mind from the very beginning of the work. The obvious place to begin the practice of self-government is in the local church. Keep in mind that the local churches form the base from which the national church will be organized. The author is firmly convinced that it is a mistake to attempt to form a national church government before there is a strong base of local churches. The establishment of strong local churches will in turn create the need for national church government and will also furnish the qualified personnel to staff this government. We should be able to look to the local church as a seedbed that produces workers.

While there are many important principles worthy of consideration concerning self-government, we will mention three.

A.   Training

The future of the national church is dependent upon the quality of leadership produced by the local churches. Paul said, "And the things that thou hast heard of me among many witnesses, the same commit thou to faithful men, who shall be able to teach others also" (II Timothy 2:2).

The work of the church is not carried on just by good men, but by *instructed men*. It is essential to train on every level including the children, which represent the leadership of the future. With the goal of self-government in view from the beginning, take steps early to establish a systematic Bible training program for developing the ministry and leadership. Someone has said that those who do not prepare for the future will not have a successful one.

The qualifications of those placed into leadership positions must be according to the Word of God. The following verses of Scripture list qualifications for church leaders that should be taught and practiced: Acts 6:3; I Timothy 3:1-13; Titus 1:5-9.

B.   Timing

Shortly after their conversion, introduce people to responsibility.

If a local church is properly organized, it will create a sense of spiritual responsibility among the members. The same is true on the national level. Self-government nurtures this sense of spiritual responsibility and helps it to spread into other areas of the church. It is out of this sense of responsibility that leaders will step forth as the need requires.

"For unto whomsoever much is given, of him shall be much required" (Luke 12:48).

Thomas Jefferson, the third president of the USA, received a letter of encouragement in 1790 that said, "Great necessities call forth great leaders."

God always has someone to fill the position:

- Israel was in Egypt   Moses
- Israel at the entrance of Canaan   Joshua
- Midian was invading the land   Gideon
- Goliath came against Israel   David
- The walls of Jerusalem had fallen   Nehemiah

The wise man Solomon said, "To every thing there is a season, and a time to every purpose under the heaven" (Ecclesiastes 3:1). This is especially true when working towards the goal of self-government. The church must maintain an atmosphere of sincere prayer and seeking after God's timing.

3.   Trust

Trust is a vital factor. An Indian proverb says, "Nothing grows under a banyan tree." A missionary has to be careful not to become too much of a dominant figure in the national church. If he allows his control of the work to overshadow that of the nationals, he can easily cripple the effect of national leadership. At the same time, he will need to maintain a certain degree of control to insure that the work is carried on properly and for the sake of training the nationals. A missionary should not hold a position in the national church that a national is able to fill. This will help to develop the ability and ministry of the nationals.

Jesus set the example that we should all follow in entrusting the work into the hands of others. Before choosing the Twelve, He spent all night in prayer (Luke 6:12-13). After choosing them, and knowing that one of them would betray Him, He spent three and one-half years with them teaching them by word and example. He taught them what their work would be and then entrusted them with the task of evangelizing the world and governing His church. What an example of trust!

Trust is the oil that lubricates the wheels of relationships and organizations and keeps them working smoothly with a minimum amount of friction.

The church must produce its own leaders. This is true for both natural and spiritual reasons. Natural reasons include language, customs, and climate, all of which make it difficult for an outsider to fit in. Spiritually, if the church strives for maturity, she will not find it necessary to depend on foreign workers. Two final questions. Who could better understand the needs and problems of the church in any country than the citizens of that country? And with proper training, who could better work towards taking care of needs and the solving of problems than the nationals of that country? That is indigenous thinking!

III. SELF-SUPPORT

Again, it is worthy to mention that in order to establish a self-supporting national church, we must start at the base with self-supporting local churches. Following are some reasons why we should work to establish self-supporting churches.

A. It is God's plan.

If this were the only reason given to insist on self-support, it should be sufficient. A careful study of the Old and New Testaments reveals that God's plan for the support of the ministry and the house of God is that of tithes and offerings. The tithe (10 percent) is for the support of the ministry and the offerings are for the building and upkeep of the house of God.

A study of the Acts of the Apostles should convince anyone that this was the apostolic method. We find no record of the mother church at Jerusalem supporting the new church plants among the Gentiles. The churches that Paul established were obviously self-supporting congregations. Paul wrote, "Even so hath the Lord ordained that they which preach the gospel should live of the gospel" (I Corinthians 9:14).

B. It is logical and practical.

An example that has often been used in teaching the logical aspect of self-support is that if there are ten or more families that tithe faithfully, they can support a pastor at the same level at which they themselves live. For example: 10 X 10 percent = 100 percent.

C. Faith and sacrifice are necessary elements in the spiritual development of the pastor and members.

Jerry Richardson, a son of pioneer missionaries and himself a missionary to Madagascar for over twenty years and former regional director for the Africa Region, related the following true story.

As a boy in the Philippines, he watched his father teach the poor people in a certain village the principle of tithing. At first these people did not have shoes, sufficient clothing to wear, and hardly enough to eat. Tithe envelopes were purchased and distributed to the people and the people began to give. The amount of their tithe at first was not even enough to pay the cost of the envelopes much less support the pastor. However, as time went by, he noticed that the people began to wear shoes to church, then their clothing improved, and soon some men were wearing ties and nice shirts. Obviously, the living conditions of the people progressively improved because they were cheerfully giving in obedience to the Word of God.

"Bring ye all the tithes into the storehouse, that there may be meat in mine house, and prove me now herewith, saith the LORD of hosts, if I will not open you the windows of heaven, and pour you out a blessing, that there shall not be room enough to receive it" (Malachi 3:10).

D. **The pastor should feel responsible to the congregation rather than to the missionary.**

In order for the necessary relationship to exist between the pastor and the congregation, it is vital for the people to feel a responsibility to their pastor and for the pastor to feel a responsibility to them. This will not happen if the missionary supports the pastor. If the pastor receives his livelihood from the missionary, he will obviously feel responsible to the missionary and not to the congregation. On the other hand, the pastor who is supported by his church will sense a close tie with the people and the people with him.

E. **Self-support helps to place the pastor in good standing with his own people.**

A pastor who is supported financially by the missionary will usually be looked upon by his own people as being an employee of a foreign organization. He will lack the respect due him as a man of God and be seen as an agent of a foreign religion, preaching a strange doctrine because he receives a salary to do so.

F. **Self-support opens the door to unlimited expansion.**

The funds that a missionary brings into a country are always limited. He works with a fixed budget that depends upon pledges that were made by churches in his homeland. If the national church depends upon these funds to operate, it will quickly come to a standstill. The day will come when no more workers can be sent out, no more new churches established, evangelism will be capped, and progress will cease. The indigenous church, on the other hand, has no such limits. It depends upon the funds generated by the national churches. As they increase in number, the funds also increase, the more it spreads, and the more it can spread. The church must be trained in independence rather than dependence.

Only people who accept and fulfill their God-given responsibilities can reach the goal of establishing the indigenous church. The salvation of God brings authority and privilege to the born again Christian. However, authority and privilege are always accompanied by responsibility. The exercise of authority or privilege, with the neglect of responsibility, leads to a false concept of reality. For example, consider when the members of a local assembly enjoy the privileges of full membership without understanding and accepting their responsibility of maintaining a place of worship and supporting their pastor. Such behavior leads to a false concept that they should always be on the receiving end with no obligation to give. Jesus said it is more blessed to give than to receive (Acts 20:35).

Every individual who has experienced forgiveness of sin, baptism in the name of Jesus, and the infilling of the Holy Ghost has a responsibility to the mission of world evangelism. This can only be accomplished by self-propagating, self-governing, and self-supporting churches. Amen.

WHAT HAVE YOU LEARNED?

Give short answers to the following questions.

1. What seemed to be Paul's favorite analogy in describing the church?

   _____

   _____

   _____

2. What two things must be kept in focus while working towards the establishment of an indigenous church?
   A. _____
   B. _____

3. Give a clear, concise definition of the local church.

_____

_____

_____

4. What is the most convincing reason for the church to be self-propagating?

_____

_____

_____

5. Why must self-government begin on the local level?

_____

_____

_____

6. When should a new convert be introduced to responsibility in the church?

_____

_____

_____

7. Why is trust an important factor in self-government?

_____

_____

_____

8. What is the plan of God for the support of the church?

_____

_____

_____

9. Name two necessary elements in spiritual development.
   A. _____
   B. _____

10. If the pastor is supported by the missionary, what problems are likely to arise? _____

_____

_____

_____

_____

Personal Study Notes

Lesson 8

The Burden and the Vision for the Harvest

Key Verse

"Say not ye, There are yet four months, and then cometh harvest? behold, I say unto you, Lift up your eyes, and look on the fields; for they are white already to harvest" (John 4:35).

Lesson Goal

To show that both a burden and a vision are necessary elements in order to see a harvest of souls on the mission field

WHAT I HAVE LEARNED

After a long, exhausting morning, the disciples left their Master sitting on the curbing of Jacob's well at Sychar and went into the city to buy food. John 4:7-26 records the conversation that followed between Jesus and a Samaritan woman. We look on as thirsty spectators as Jesus talks about living water that would forever quench the thirst of weary souls and then as He reveals Himself as the long-awaited Messiah to a woman of ill repute. As His disciples return they are quite amazed that He would converse with this heathen but quickly pass it off as they hastily seek to fill their empty stomachs. Someone blurts out, "Master, eat." And then, as from another world, Jesus answers, "I have meat to eat that ye know not of." Hesitating between bites for a few quick words, they ask if someone has brought Him food in their absence.

Jesus responds: "My meat is to do the will of him that sent me, and to finish his work. Say not ye, There are yet four months, and then cometh harvest? behold, I say unto you, Lift up your eyes, and look on the fields; for they are white already to harvest" (John 4:34-35).

These words will serve as a reference point for this lesson on the burden and vision for the harvest. At this point in the Scriptures, the disciples did not comprehend the purpose for which Christ had come into the world. They were not feeling the burden of His heart for a lost world, and neither were they seeing what He saw when He looked at the crowds.

I.　UNDERSTANDING THE PURPOSE OF THE INCARNATION

A story was told of a young lad who was proudly strolling through his village showing everyone the bird in his cage that he had recently snared. An old man met him and asked if he could take a closer look at the caged bird. Of course, the boy was happy to show the old man his new captive. After taking a long, careful look at the bird, the old man asked the boy if he would sell it. Surprised that the old man was interested, the boy quickly responded yes and quoted his price. The old man reached deep into his pocket and counted out the exact amount of money into a dirty little hand. Then ever so carefully, the old man reached into the cage, took the frightened bird into his gentle hand, and removed it from the cage. After examining the bird, the old man raised his hand high into the air and released the bird. Flapping its wings frantically, the bird quickly flew away across the fields to freedom. The boy quickly asked the old man, "Why did you do that?" The old man calmly answered, "When it was your bird, you kept it in the cage; I paid the price for the bird so I could set it free."

This was the purpose of the birth of the Christ in Bethlehem, the Lamb of God, which takes away the sin of the world (John 1:29). He came to preach the gospel to the poor, to heal the brokenhearted, to preach deliverance to the captives, and recovering of sight to the blind, to set at liberty them that are bruised (Luke 4:18). He came to seek and to save that which was lost (Luke 19:10). He came to give His life a ransom for many (Mark 10:45). There is no real freedom without the freedom from sin.

Until we understand this purpose, we cannot:

- Feel the burden for a lost world for which He died.
- Sense the urgent need to go into the fields.
- See the vision of a ripened harvest that waits.

II. HOW TO RECEIVE A BURDEN

A. Give.

It has been proven repeatedly that a real burden for the harvest manifests itself through consistent giving to world missions.

As has been previously stated, an important factor taken into consideration by the Global Missions Board of the United Pentecostal Church International when considering an application for missionary appointment, is the candidate's history of giving. Has he or she expressed a genuine burden for world missions by a consistent giving of finances?

This can also be seen as we look at the early church. Many good things can be said of the church that was at Antioch. It was at Antioch where the disciples were first called Christians. Prophets were in the church at Antioch, the Holy Ghost spoke frequently through the church at Antioch, and Jews and Gentiles worshiped together at Antioch.

One notable thing about this church was that the people gave liberally. Acts 11:29-30 says the disciples at Antioch gave special love offerings to send to the church at Jerusalem. However, Antioch is by far best known for its missionary involvement. Antioch seems to have been solely responsible for the sending of Paul and Barnabas on their first missionary journey. As well, Paul based all of his missionary work from this church. It is reasonable to believe that this church provided special funds for the purpose of world evangelism.

Giving to a cause promotes a feeling of being involved, and this gives way to the birth of a burden for that cause.

B. Pray.

One of the easiest and quickest ways to visit a foreign land is on our knees in prayer. Spread out a world map, and in a matter of an hour's time, you can visit every nation on planet earth. National boundaries cannot stop prayer. You can visit nations that are hostile to Christianity while in the safety of your home. Prayer changes things but prayer also changes people. Most noticeably, prayer changes the one who prays. An individual cannot sincerely pray day after day for the harvest without being greatly affected day after day by an increasing burden for the harvest.

An important part of praying for the harvest is that of making yourself available to God. Saul of Tarsus (later Paul), with his face in the sand on the Damascus road, responded to the voice of the Lord by saying, "Lord, what wilt thou have me to do?" (Acts 9:6). He was in essence saying, "Lord, I'll do what you want me to do; I'll go where you want me to go." God will use what is made available to Him. It could be a handful of meal in a barrel, five loaves of bread, two small fish, a Saul of Tarsus, or you and me. Paul said in Romans 12:1 that we should present our bodies a living sacrifice unto God to prove, among other things, what the will of God for our lives is.

C.   Take a new look at the Crucifixion.

Read Isaiah 53 carefully. Place yourself in the Scriptures. For example: "He was wounded for my transgressions." And then put the masses of lost humanity in the Scriptures. Example: "He was wounded for their transgressions." The intention is not to change the Word of God but to draw our attention to the purpose of the crucifixion of Jesus Christ. Read carefully again the account of the crucifixion in Matthew, Mark, Luke, and John. Consider the heathen population of this world in the light of John 3:16; Romans 5:6-8; I John 3:16 and many others. Visit Calvary again in your prayers.

The death of the Jesus Christ on the cross exhibited the greatest expression of the love of God for humankind. "Greater love hath no man than this, that a man lay down his life for his friends" (John 15:13). Let the love of God flow from Calvary through your heart unto the world for which the Savior died. While kneeling there in contrition, gaze upon the harvest fields, allowing the Holy Ghost to push forth a well of compassion from your innermost being. A sincere heart cannot remain unmoved in this atmosphere.

Reflect on the words of a song by George Bennard:

On a hill far away stood an old rugged cross,
The emblem of suffering and shame;
And I love that old cross where the dearest and best
For a world of lost sinners was slain.

D.   Look upon the fields.

Jesus said, "Lift up your eyes, and look on the fields." It is a natural tendency for us to focus our attention upon our own personal needs and problems. At times all we see is that small area of life called "self." However, if there is to be a burden for the harvest, we must look beyond self, beyond home, and fix our eyes upon the masses of unevangelized people in other villages, cities, nations, and regions. Jesus said the field is the world (Matthew 13:38) and looking on the field helps to create a genuine burden and concern for souls. Receiving letters and reports from missionaries in other countries can be very inspiring. This can be arranged through the national headquarters or through the Global Missions in North America.

III.   WHAT DO YOU SEE WHEN YOU LOOK AT PEOPLE?

A.   Jesus saw their sufferings.

"And great multitudes came unto him, having with them those that were lame, blind, dumb, maimed, and many others, and cast them down at Jesus' feet; and he healed them" (Matthew 15:30).

B.   Jesus saw their tears.

"And when the Lord saw her, he had compassion on her, and said unto her, Weep not" (Luke 7:13).

C.   Jesus e saw their fears.

"But straightway Jesus spake unto them, saying, Be of good cheer; it is I; be not afraid" (Matthew 14:27).

D.   Jesus saw their need of forgiveness.

"And he said unto her, Thy sins are forgiven" (Luke 7:48).

E.   Jesus saw their desire for the Word of God.

"And it came to pass, that, as the people pressed upon him to hear the word of God, he stood by the lake of Gennesaret" (Luke 5:1).

F.   Jesus saw their faith.

"When Jesus saw their faith, he said unto the sick of the palsy, Son, thy sins be forgiven thee" (Mark 2:5).

G.   Jesus saw them through eyes of compassion.

"I have compassion on the multitude, because they have now been with me three days, and have nothing to eat" (Mark 8:2).

H.   Jesus saw them as sheep having no shepherd.

"And Jesus, when he came out, saw much people, and was moved with compassion toward them, because they were as sheep not having a shepherd" (Mark 6:34).

What do you see when you look at people?

Jesus stood on a hillside and wept over the city of Jerusalem as He considered the inhabitants' dilemma (Luke 19:41). The spiritual condition of Jeremiah's people so grieved him that he cried, "Oh that my head were waters, and mine eyes a fountain of tears, that I might weep day and night for the slain of the daughter of my people" (Jeremiah 9:1).

While in the city of Bethsaida, people brought a blind man to Jesus for healing. After He had spit on his eyes and put His hands upon him, Jesus asked him if he could see. The man responded that he saw men as trees walking. Jesus put His hands on his eyes a second time and made him look up. After this second touch, he saw every man clearly (Mark 8:22-25). We should pray for the Lord to touch our eyes again that we might see all men clearly through eyes of compassion.

IV.   A VISION FOR THE HARVEST

Without doubt, the greatest promise in the Bible pertaining to end-time harvest is that of Joel 2:28-32, which Peter quoted on the Day of Pentecost.

"And it shall come to pass in the last days, saith God, I will pour out of my Spirit upon all flesh" (Acts 2:17).

This promise removes all limits of race and nationality. The only limits to this promise are to those who do not believe it.

A.   What is a vision as it pertains to the church?

A vision is a clear and preferable mental image of the future of the church as its leadership believes it can and must be.

Do not confuse the *mission of the church* with a *vision for the church*. They are both vitally important to success but very different in meaning.

Mission: describes why the church exists.
Vision: describes where the church is going in the future with the mission.

B.   How do you receive a vision?

In his book *Developing the Leader Within You*, John Maxwell gives six guidelines on how to receive a vision:

1. Look within you: What do you feel?
2. Look behind you: What have you learned?
3. Look around you: What is happening to others?
4. Look ahead of you: What is the big picture?
5. Look above you: What does God expect of you?
6. Look beside you: What resources are available?[4]

"Whereby are given unto us exceeding great and precious promises" (II Peter 1:4).

God prepared a garden for Adam. He promised Noah that his family would be saved in the ark. For Abraham there was a promised son (Isaac) and a

---

[4] John Maxwell, *Developing the Leader Within You* (Nashville: Thomas Nelson, Inc., 1993 by Injoy Inc.), 145-148.

promised land (Canaan). This same country was promised to Isaac, Jacob, Moses, Joshua, and Israel. However, to the church, the promise is exceeding great and precious. God has promised the whole world: "all flesh." There are no physical or cultural boundaries; race, age, and social status are not factors. The harvest is ripe and plentiful, but the great shortage is of laborers. Let us bend our knees and bow our hearts in prayer. Let us place our shoulder under the cross and bear a burden. Let us lift up our eyes and look on the fields that are white already to harvest. And let us go and work while it is yet day for the night cometh when no man can work. Amen.

What Have You Learned?

Give short answers to the following questions.

1. What was the "meat" spoken of by Jesus in John 4:34?

_____

_____

_____

2. What was the purpose of the Incarnation?

_____

_____

_____

3. Why is a good understanding of the Incarnation necessary?

_____

_____

_____

4. Explain what is meant by a "burden for the harvest."

_____

_____

_____

5. Name four things that will help someone receive a burden.
    A. _____
    B. _____
    C. _____
    D. _____

6. Name some things that Jesus saw when He looked at people?
    _____
    _____
    _____
    _____

7. What is significant about Joel 2:28?
    _____
    _____
    _____

8. Define *vision* as it pertains to the church.
    _____
    _____
    _____

9. Explain the difference between *mission* and *vision*.
    _____
    _____
    _____
    _____

10. How do you receive a vision for the harvest?
    _____
    _____
    _____
    _____
    _____

Personal Study Notes

Lesson 9

What Is the Missionary Call?

Key Verse

"As they ministered to the Lord, and fasted, the Holy Ghost said, Separate me Barnabas and Saul for the work whereunto I have called them" (Acts 13:2).

Lesson Goal

To establish a scriptural point of view of the call of God and to know how to recognize the call of a missionary

WHAT I HAVE LEARNED

The word *call* is used in various ways in the New Testament. Most often it refers to the Christian life and not service that would pertain to the ministry. In Acts 2:39, after giving the requirements for salvation, Peter said the promise of the Holy Ghost "is unto you, and to your children, and to all that are afar off, even as many as the Lord our God shall call." Obviously, Peter was not saying that God calls everyone into the ministry but that everyone is called to repentance, baptism in Jesus' name for the remission of sins, and to receive the Holy Ghost. This constitutes the universal call to salvation.

There is, however, a definite call to Christian service on a full-time basis, which would include apostles, prophets, evangelists, pastors, and teachers

(Ephesians 4:11). From among these areas of ministry some receive a special call to go into other cities, regions, and countries to announce the gospel to those who have never heard. They go and establish the New Testament church according to the pattern in the Word of God. These men and women are missionaries who have been called and sent into the harvest by the Lord of the harvest.

A.   Characteristics of Some Who Were Called

We will consider seven men who received a definite call of God in the Word of God. In each example, certain characteristics seem to have dominated their lives. Some of them possessed all of the qualities that will be listed, but others only a few. A dominant trait seems to have been in each of them. Our goal is to show that if some or all of these same characteristics are present in an individual today, he or she may be a candidate for the call of God to service.

1.   Abraham → Faith in God

From his entrance onto the pages of the Bible until his exit, Abraham walked by faith. His faith was tested many times. "For what saith the scripture? Abraham believed God, and it was counted unto him for righteousness" (Romans 4:3). The writer of Hebrews also speaks of the call of Abraham: "By faith Abraham, when he was called to go out . . . went out, not knowing whither he went" (Hebrews 11:8).

2.   Moses → Obedience to God

When you look at the life of Moses, you see that he regularly received commandments from God and was quite thorough carrying out of those orders. "Go tell Pharaoh . . . Go tell the children of Israel . . . Throw the rod on the ground . . . Stretch the rod out . . . Smite the rock . . . Gather the manna each day . . . Build a tabernacle . . .", and so forth. And he obeyed the voice of the Lord.

3.   Gideon → Courage

This "mighty man of valor" was called to deliver his people from the hands of Midian. It took courage to go with only three hundred men to face an army that was compared in number to grasshoppers. Courage increases in the life of a leader at the same rate as the importance of the mission. If he sees his mission as being great, his courage will increase to meet the challenge. On the other hand, if the mission is not important to the leader, he will lack the courage to endure hardships in the pursuit of the mission. True courage will always be challenged.

4.   Elisha → Hard Work

The call of God to Elisha was unexpected. Elijah did not find him in the school of the prophets but in the field ploughing (I Kings 19:19). He must have been quite a successful man to have owned land, oxen, and servants. Yet Elisha did not think it a disgrace to put his own hands to the plough. He was a hard-working farmer.

> Idleness is no man's honor, nor is husbandry any man's disgrace.

Were not Peter, James, and John busy fishermen when called by Jesus? Matthew was a tax collector and Luke a doctor. God calls hard-working men.

5.   Isaiah → Willingness/Availability

Some say that Isaiah was a courtyard prophet, well acquainted with royalty, wealth, and affluence. But he was not called based on these impressive qualities.

It was after the death of proud King Uzziah that Isaiah saw the vision of the Lord upon His throne. During this vision of the glory of God, Isaiah "heard the voice of the Lord, saying, whom shall I send, and who will go for us?" His response was "Here am I; send me" (Isaiah 6:8). Simply stated, Isaiah had a vision, heard a voice, saw a need, and volunteered. Availability is indispensable to receiving the call of God.

6.   Jeremiah → Burden/Passion for His People

The "Weeping Prophet" was called into service at a young tender age. When he heard the voice of the Lord he responded, "I cannot speak: for I am a child" (Jeremiah 1:6). His lifetime of ministry is well marked by a stream of tears he shed for his people. He prophesied of the backsliding, bondage, and restoration of the Jews. He was rejected by his neighbors, family, other priests, and prophets, his friends, and by the king. He was put in stocks in a miry dungeon and carried captive into Egypt. An undying burden and passion for the Jewish nation characterized His call.

7.   Paul → Self-denial/Personal Sacrifice

Much could be said about Paul. He was from a very prominent background. He was circumcised the eighth day, of the stock of Israel, of the tribe of Benjamin, an Hebrew of the Hebrews; as touching the law, a Pharisee; concerning zeal, persecuting the church; touching the righteousness which is in the law, blameless (Philippians 3:5-6). Furthermore, he was brought up at the feet of Gamaliel, possibly the most sought after rabbi of that day, and taught according to the perfect manner of the law of the fathers (Acts 22:3). And yet the following statement echoes throughout the ministry of the apostle to the Gentiles:

> "But what things were gain to me, those I counted loss for Christ. Yea doubtless, and I count all things but loss for the excellency of the knowledge of Christ Jesus my Lord: for whom I have suffered the loss of all things, and do count them but dung, that I may win Christ" (Philippians 3:7-8).

Of all these men, none was perfect, and no one is perfect today. But there were obvious characteristics in their lives that were of particular interest to God. He chose them. He called them. He sent them. He equipped them and they said yes.

II. PREREQUISITES FOR RECEIVING A CALL

In his book, *Life and Work on the Mission Field*, J. Herbert Kane suggests that one who is going to be called must meet the following conditions:

A. An Open Mind

We must be absolutely honest with God, our leadership, and ourselves. We must keep all options open and allow the Holy Ghost to take full control of our mental faculties (II Corinthians 10:5).

B. An Attentive Ear

We must keep our ears open to the voice of the Lord. We must train ourselves to hear His slightest whisper. This sensitivity is developed only through a consecrated prayer life.

C. A Pure Heart

God reveals His truth, not to those who want to know it, but to those who want to do it. Holiness is required by God (I Peter 1:16). Only the pure in heart will stand in His holy place and see Him (Psalm 24:3-4; Matthew 5:8).

D.   Busy Hands

An old axiom states, "Idle hands are the devil's workshop." The call of God comes to those who are busy like Moses, David, Elisha, Peter, James, John, and so on. He seeks workers, not lazy people, to labor in His vineyard (Proverbs 13:4; 20:4). Any person feeling a call should get busy doing something for the Lord.

E.   Ready Feet

"How beautiful upon the mountains are the feet of him that bringeth good tidings, that publisheth peace; that bringeth good tidings of good, that publisheth salvation; that saith unto Zion, Thy God reigneth!" (Isaiah 52:7). The time is short and the King's business requires haste (I Corinthians 7:29; I Samuel 21:8). Indecision and procrastination are enemies of the call of God.

III.   STEPS IN RECOGNIZING THE CALL

Usually a call is a developing process that may take months, even years to come to full fruition. However, along the way are some well-defined stages that are helpful in recognizing the call. These include the following (based on "Recognizing a Call" in *Life and Word on the Mission Field* by J. Herbert Kane):

A.   Curiosity

This may come through a book, conversation, friend, or speaker. The person may be completely unaware.

B.   Interest

Turning repeatedly to the subject that has caught his attention.

C.   Understanding

One begins to understand the nature, scope, meaning, and mandate of the mission: lost man, the unfinished task, and the opportunity for service.

D.   Assurance

One's heart is strangely warmed and he begins to feel assured.

E.   Conviction

He feels that he must be a missionary or a preacher.

F.   Commitment

He is ready to sign the Princeton Pledge: "I purpose, God willing, to be a missionary."

G.   Action

He plans and goes where his heart is; and where his heart is, his feet will follow.

These seven steps involve the whole man. The first three involve the mind, the next three involve the heart, and the last one involves the will.

IV.   MAKING YOUR CALLING AND ELECTION SURE

To conclude this lesson, we look at II Peter 1:5-10. These verses begin and end by exhorting us to use all diligence in the interest of making our calling and election sure. It is understood that this exhortation is not given uniquely for the ministry but for all believers. However, it is certainly applicable for those who sense that God is calling them into a special area of service. The practice of these guidelines will be helpful to the individual who sincerely seeks to please the Lord. These verses give seven spiritual building blocks to add to the foundation of our faith.

1. Virtue
2. Knowledge
3. Temperance
4. Patience
5. Godliness
6. Brotherly kindness
7. Charity

Notice carefully verses 8-10:

"For if these things be in you, and abound, they make you that ye shall neither be barren nor unfruitful in the knowledge of our Lord Jesus Christ. But he that lacketh these things is blind, and cannot see afar off, and hath forgotten that he was purged from his old sins. Wherefore the rather, brethren, give diligence to make your calling and election sure: for if ye do these things, ye shall never fall" (II Peter 1:8-10).

What Have You Learned?

Give short answers to the following questions.

1. What is the difference between the universal call of God to salvation and His call to service?

   _____

   _____

   _____

2. What one characteristic seemed to dominate the life and calling of
   A. Abraham _____
   B. Moses _____
   C. Gideon _____
   D. Elisha _____
   E. Jeremiah _____
   F. Paul _____

3. List five prerequisites for receiving a call.
   A. _____
   B. _____
   C. _____
   D. _____
   E. _____

4. Explain in your own words, how to recognize the call of God.

_____
_____
_____
_____

5. Write a paragraph and explain the calling of a missionary.

_____
_____
_____
_____
_____
_____
_____
_____
_____
_____
_____

Lesson 10

What Are the Prerequisites of Being a Missionary and Doing Missionary Work?

Key Verse

"For he was a good man, and full of the Holy Ghost and of faith: and much people was added unto the Lord" (Acts 11:24).

Lesson Goal

To determine the prerequisites of becoming a missionary, to show why they are important to the work, and to understand that there must be a time of preparation beforehand.

WHAT I HAVE LEARNED

From the very beginning, following the new birth experience, the believer should be taught the importance of self-preparation for involvement in the mission of the church. Salvation is like a journey, and the new birth is the starting point. This is especially true of an individual who is feeling the call of God upon his or her life. Even before it is clear what area of ministry the calling is for, preparation should be set in motion early. Someone said, "What you are going to be tomorrow, you are becoming today."

The coach of a basketball team that was undefeated during the regular season and went on to win the national championship was asked what the key to the success of the team was. "Was it the will to succeed?" he was asked. The coach replied, "The will to succeed is important, but what is more important is the will to prepare." If training and preparation are important to the success of a sports team, how much more important are they to the success of the ministry of a missionary in a foreign country. Let it be understood that the prerequisites given in this lesson are basic Christian characteristics that can be developed in a day-by-day walk of faith and obedience to the Word of God, a life of prayer and consecration, and the practice of self-discipline.

I. MUST BE BORN AGAIN

This may sound elementary, but the new birth experience constitutes the very entrance into the kingdom of God (John 3:3-8). Jesus made it very clear in His teachings that to be born again of water and of the Spirit is necessary and not optional. How can someone teach others the way of salvation if he himself has not had the experience?

Notice carefully the following paragraph taken from the UPCI Global Missions manual: "The candidate shall have the personal experience of full New Testament salvation according to our fundamental doctrine (Acts 2:38), namely, repentance of sins, baptism in water in the name of Jesus Christ for the remission of sins and the receiving of the gift of the Holy Ghost, evidenced by speaking with other tongues as the Spirit gives utterance. Said candidates must believe this to be essential to salvation" (*Global Missions Manual of the United Pentecostal Church International*, page 30, 2015 revision).

II. THE CALL OF GOD

Many wrong motives exist for entering missionary service: the desire to travel, seeking personal glory, seeking freedom from authority, ineffectiveness at home, just to name a few. However, the proper motivation is the call of God with a sincere desire to fulfill the will of God by reaching a lost world. We have studied in previous lessons the importance of the call and how to recognize it.

We would do well to notice again that while at Antioch, Paul and Barnabas were called by the Holy Ghost to go to the mission field. The church then recognized their call. The elders laid their hands on them, prayed for them, and sent them away. This was all considered the work of the Holy Ghost (Acts 13:1-4). The importance of the church recognizing the call of God in someone's life should not be overlooked. The church has the responsibility of sending to the field those whom the Lord has called.

III. A BURDEN FOR THE LOST

Of necessity, a sincere burden to see the lost saved must be within the heart. When Jesus spoke of the shepherd who left the ninety-nine sheep to go in search of the one lost lamb, He said that he will "go after that which is lost, until he find it" (Luke 15:4). He said of the woman that had ten pieces of silver and lost one of them that she would "seek diligently till she find it" (Luke 15:8). What would cause the shepherd to search without ceasing until he finds the lost lamb? What would drive the woman to search tirelessly every inch of the house with light and broom until she has found the lost piece? The answer is found in a deep-seated desire and passion to recover what was lost.

This is comparable to the burden that must be present in a candidate for missionary service. It is because of a burden that he or she will leave behind familiar comforts. They will search for those precious lost souls for which Christ died. This burden will not leave them at peace until they have brought that which was lost within reach of the compassionate Savior.

IV. PROVEN FAITHFUL IN THE CHURCH

A. To the Local Church and Pastor

It is imperative that the candidates for missions service be proven faithful in their local churches and to their pastors. The endorsement of the pastor will be necessary. If people have not been faithful in the local church and to their pastors, how can they be trusted to be faithful in a faraway land? Faithfulness begins at home with small things (Luke 16:10).

B. To the Organization with Which He Works

To have the endorsement of the organization, the candidate must have worked in faithful cooperation with other ministers and with those in leadership positions. He must have proven himself trustworthy in doctrinal as well as spiritual matters, keeping in mind that those who will support his endeavors abroad will likely be his fellow ministers.

C.   Live a Consistent, Consecrated Life

Paul said "every man that striveth for the mastery is temperate in all things" (I Corinthians 9:25). He was speaking of an athlete disciplining himself while in training for the race. He went on to say that they do this to receive a corruptible crown, but we as Christians exercise self-discipline in order to receive an incorruptible crown. Paul wrote to the Christians at Rome, saying, "Present your bodies a living sacrifice, holy, acceptable unto God, which is your reasonable service" (Romans 12:1).

Notice he said for you to present your bodies. This requires self-discipline. This practice should be put into action early in the life of an individual born again into the kingdom of God. If bad habits are made, rest assured good habits can also be made. The mission field is not the place to work out personal convictions of holiness. Many other things there will demand one's time and energy. An individual must be well settled in this area. He should also have an unquestionable moral character. If an individual has a history of immoral conduct since his conversion, the mission field could be detrimental for him and he could greatly hinder the work.

D.   Practice Faithful Stewardship

Concerning Christian stewardship, faithfulness is the key, and honesty must be at the heart of it all. Paul said, "It is required in stewards, that a man be found faithful" (I Corinthians 4:2). Notice that it is *not suggested* but *required* that a steward be found faithful.

Again, this must start at home. A minister who is not faithful at home, will not be faithful abroad. If he has not maintained a faithful practice of tithing and giving in offerings at home, he will not be able effectively to teach these important principles of the Word of God on the mission field. If he has not proven himself a faithful steward with money at home, he will not be trustworthy in a foreign land. If he has not shown faithfulness with his own finances in his local church, he will not show faithfulness with the financial support of other churches that would send him to the mission field. He must be honest with God, his fellowman, and with himself.

E.   Personal Prayer Life

The space given here is not sufficient to cover this important subject. From day one after conversion, individuals should begin to develop their personal prayer life with special times set aside for daily prayer. Prayer can be taught. One can preach about prayer. Much reading material on the subject of prayer is available, but prayer must be practiced to be effective.

Prayer is direct communication with God. Prayer is powerful. Prayer moves God to work on the behalf of the church. Prayer changes things, but the most important thing that prayer changes is the person who is praying. Praying in groups is good, praying with other saints is needful; but nothing takes the place of being alone with the Lord, pouring out one's heart upon a personal altar of prayer. It is very easy to neglect personal prayer on the mission field. Therefore, this habit must be developed while at home.

V.   SOUND IN DOCTRINE

It has been said, "He who stands for nothing will fall for anything." A missionary must be well settled in what he believes. Many strange doctrines run rampant in the earth today. Paul said, "In the latter times some shall depart from the faith, giving heed to seducing spirits, and doctrines of devils" (I Timothy 4:1). It is certain that a missionary will encounter these and many other situations on the field. He must preach and insist upon the new birth experience as is recorded in Acts 2:38, as a necessity of salvation. Before he can effectively preach and teach the apostolic doctrine, he must first believe it himself.

The following statement referring to candidates for Global Missions service is taken from *the UPCI Global Missions Manual (2015)*, page 30: "Said candidates shall believe this to be essential to salvation. They shall believe, practice, and teach the fundamental doctrine and the Articles of Faith of the United Pentecostal Church International."

> "And they continued stedfastly in the apostles' doctrine" (Acts 2:42).

VI.   MUST UNDERSTAND THE OBJECTIVES OF THE WORK

Much time, money, and many precious souls can be lost if the missionary does not have a good understanding of the objectives that he or she is working to accomplish. It is suggested that every candidate for missions service study carefully the indigenous church principles before going to the field. Some good books are available on this subject. The primary objective for every missionary should be to establish in the country of his labor, the New Testament church based upon the practice of New Testament church principles.

VII. UNDERSTAND RESPONSIBILITY AND THE PROPER USE OF AUTHORITY

Responsibility follows blessings and responsibility brings authority. The abuse of either of these can cause serious problems in the work of God.

A. Responsibility

Many times the call of God to the mission field carries with it the responsibility of reaching an entire nation with the gospel of Jesus Christ. This is a two-fold responsibility: (1) to the Lord and (2) to the world for which He died. Every Christian will one day give account of his responsibilities to the Lord. This should never be taken lightly but rather with the utmost of sincerity.

Then there is the responsibility to the organization. Again, accountability is a key word. The missionary must maintain a good rapport with the pastors and churches that have sent him to the field. He must understand his responsibility in this area. A good, clear, and honest record is of utmost importance. Whether it is finances or statistics, honesty is the best policy.

B. Proper Use of Authority

The abuse of authority in the church has led to the downfall of many good men and all this in the name of religion. Authority can be compared to a loaded gun. If it is put to the head or turned toward oneself and discharged, it can be deadly. In the same way if authority is used for personal gain, personal glory, or for personal power struggles, it will surely bring spiritual injury or death to those involved. A careful study and application of I Peter 5:2-4 is helpful here.

VIII. WILLING TO WORK IN HARMONY WITH OTHERS

The key word here is *teamwork*. The Bible provides many illustrations of the power of unity. In Genesis 11, the builders of the tower of Babel displayed unity and teamwork, and the Lord said their goal would be accomplished even though they were working contrary to the will of God. In Acts 2, unity in the upper room on the Day of Pentecost resulted in the Holy Ghost being poured out. Throughout the Book of Acts, we see unity, cooperation, and teamwork in the day-to-day operation of the New Testament church. This was according to the perfect will of God. One only has to look to the pages of history to see the importance of solidarity in the accomplishment of great tasks. No greater or more important task is in the world than the accomplishment of the Great Commission of the Lord Jesus Christ.

A willingness to work in harmony and unity with other men is essential if this mission is to be accomplished. Whether it is with nationals or fellow missionaries, one must be willing to work with others. Likewise, one must willingly work with and under the authority of the established leadership in the organization. Once again it is worthy of mention that this must begin at home in the local church setting.

IX.   ADJUST TO CHANGE AND BE IN GOOD HEALTH

A.   Adjusting to Change

Perhaps one of the most trying areas of missionary work is that of adjusting to different cultures. This depends largely upon the fields involved. The candidate must be willing to accept a lower standard of living than his own, if necessary, for the cause of Christ. It is likely that the food and eating habits will be different from those to which he is accustomed. Many times the climate will be different from at home. He can expect language barriers, social differences, and traditions other than his own. These adjustments can be stressful for the missionary, for his family, and for the people with whom he is working. Patience and much prayer are necessary.

B.   Good Health

Obviously, because of the many changes they will face, the candidates must be in reasonably good health. The availability of proper medical help and facilities can be lacking on many fields. Common illnesses can become deadly enemies.

The threat of different viruses and fevers is in different lands. Therefore, good eating habits, plenty of rest, and exercise are necessary practices to maintain a healthy body. Paul stated that the body is the temple of God and that we should take care not to defile His temple (I Corinthians 3:16-17).

X.   Have Some Leadership Qualities

Perhaps it would be unjust to make a list of leadership qualities and state that each is essential for missionary work. However, it is fair to say that a candidate for missionary work must have the ability to lead people if he is going to accomplish his task. His ability to lead people in the right direction will surely determine the success or failure of his mission. It is true that if God calls an individual, He will also qualify that individual. However, the man who desires to make his calling and election sure as a missionary would do well to give some time to the development of leadership skills before going to the field. Both Moses and David were shepherds before they were leaders of God's people. There was obviously a time of preparation. Again, much can be accomplished in this area in the local church setting.

WHAT HAVE YOU LEARNED?

Give short answers to the following questions.

1. What does the *UPCI Global Missions Manual* state concerning the candidate for Global Missions service and the new birth experience?

    _____

    _____

    _____

    _____

2. Name some wrong motives for entering Global Missions service.

    _____

    _____

    _____

3. Describe the correct motive for entering Global Missions service.

_____

_____

_____

4. Explain why a burden is a prerequisite to Global Missions service.

_____

_____

_____

5. Name five areas of faithfulness in the church that are important prerequisites to Global Missions service.

A. _____

B. _____

C. _____

D. _____

E. _____

6. Why is soundness in doctrine important?

_____

_____

_____

7. What should be the primary objective of every missionary?

_____

_____

_____

_____

8. What is the two-fold responsibility of every Christian including the missionary?

A. _____

B. _____

9. What is the usual result of the abuse of authority in the church?

_____

_____

_____

10. What is the key word to working in harmony with others?

_____

11 Name some changes that can be difficult for the missionary on the foreign field. _____

_____

_____

_____

12. Why is it important for the person who feels the call of God to develop leadership skills? _____

_____

_____

_____

Lesson 11

What Are the Objectives of Global Missions, UPCI?

Key Verse

"After this I beheld, and, lo, a great multitude, which no man could number, of all nations, and kindreds, and people, and tongues, stood before the throne, and before the Lamb, clothed with white robes, and palms in their hands" (Revelation 7:9).

Lesson Goal

To have a clear understanding of why the United Pentecostal Church International exists and what it seeks to accomplish in the world through Global Missions.

WHAT I HAVE LEARNED

Motion and activity are not always evidence of true progress but rather at times only show our busyness. It all depends upon the direction in which we are actually moving as compared to the direction in which we should be moving. Therefore, we must have and follow a set of clearly defined objectives that will help us to maintain movement in the right direction. That is progress. It was stated in a previous lesson, "If you aim at nothing you are likely to hit nothing." Effective planning for the future is impossible without clear objectives because you have no target at which to aim. This is true on the local as well as the national level of the church.

Karl Marx ended his *Communist Manifesto* with these words, "You have a world to win." Communists believe that if they make big demands on people, they will get a big response. Marx's aim was high, but his motivation was godless and evil.

Jesus Christ ended His earthly ministry by saying, "Go ye into all the world, and preach the gospel to every creature" (Mark 16:15). He made great demands on His followers but promised to give them great grace and power to accomplish the task. His aim was the highest, and His motivation was godly and pure.

Here are five questions, which when answered, are helpful in determining our true objectives:

1. What does God want us to do?
2. Whom are we trying to reach?
3. How are we going to accomplish this?
4. Where is our geographical target?
5. What results do we anticipate?

With these in mind, we will study the objectives of the United Pentecostal Church in organizing Global Missions. The contents of this lesson are from the *UPCI Global Missions Manual.*

I. THE UNITED PENTECOSTAL CHURCH INTERNATIONAL

In 1945 two major organizations of ministers and layman embracing the doctrine and experience of Apostolic Pentecostals, as related in Acts 2, united into a body known as the United Pentecostal Church. The purpose of this church, as stated in the "Foreword" of the *United Pentecostal Church International Manual,* is "to preach the gospel of Christ Jesus; to publish and distribute religious literature; to establish new churches; *to send forth missionaries*; to perform any other duties connected with religious work, and to help in any way possible to meet the needs of local churches."

The same document further declares, "To the end we now pledge our prayers, our faith, our life and love, our earthly means of support, and our time, in the fear of God and for His glory alone."

II.   GLOBAL MISSIONS

The objective of the United Pentecostal Church International (UPCI) in organizing Global Missions is to proclaim the whole gospel to the whole world by sending forth God-called men and women in obedience to the Great Commission. "Go ye into all the world and preach the gospel to every creature" (Mark 16:15).

"The whole gospel to the whole world by the whole church."

It is further "the purpose of the United Pentecostal Church to seek out and to carry the gospel to the whole world, and to help establish self-supporting, self-governing, and self-propagating national churches" (*UPCI Manual*, Article XII, Section 1, Paragraph 1).

III.   THE ULTIMATE GOAL AND AIM

The ultimate goal of Global Missions is to prepare the church for the coming of Jesus Christ for His bride. "That he might present it to himself a glorious church, not having spot, or wrinkle, or any such thing; but that it should be holy and without blemish" (Ephesians 5:27). To this end it is the absolute responsibility of this God-instituted body to teach the oneness of the Godhead in Jesus Christ; the repentance of all sin; baptism by immersion in the name of Jesus Christ for the remission of sin; and the receiving of the Holy Ghost with the initial sign of speaking in other tongues as the Spirit gives utterance.

Thereafter it is the responsibility of the ministry to teach all baptized believers that they must "follow peace with all men, and holiness, without which no man shall see the Lord" (Hebrews 12:14).

IV.   OBJECTIVES OF GLOBAL MISSIONS

It is imperative that every missionary of the UPCI knows and understands the objectives of Global Missions. For this reason these objectives are stated as follows:

A. To send forth God-called missionaries into all the world to preach the gospel of the kingdom to every creature.

B. To train national workers and ministers that they might, in fulfillment of the Great Commission, be able to evangelize and give leadership to the churches among their own people and in missionary outreach to other nations.

C. To produce under God, self-governing, self-propagating, and self-supporting national churches in every country according to the apostolic pattern.

D. To establish an international fellowship of the United Pentecostal Church. National churches shall be encouraged to maintain the closest fraternal fellowship with the United Pentecostal Church International in the United States and Canada and with the United Pentecostal Churches worldwide.

E. To create, by the power of the Word of God and the working of the Holy Spirit, a love for truth and holiness. This love will bind the church to the heart of God and produce the bride of Christ from among every nation, tribe, and tongue in the whole world (Revelation 5:9).

Being aware of the human impossibility of the task, we put our trust in God, His power and His Word, and seek to establish a center of operations in every land from which national workers and ministers are sent forth. The missionary must be aware of the fact that he alone cannot fully accomplish that which must be done; therefore, he must pray and trust God to add to the church capable nationals who will bring to completion the full evangelization of each country and thereby the whole world.

WHAT HAVE YOU LEARNED?

Give short answers to the following questions.

1. Why must we as a church have a clearly defined objective?

   _____

   _____

   _____

2. This lesson gives five questions that help to determine our objectives as an organization. List these five questions with the answers.

   A. _____

   _____

   _____

   B. _____

   _____

   _____

   C. _____

   _____

   _____

   D. _____

   _____

   _____

   E. _____

   _____

   _____

3. State the purpose of the formation of the United Pentecostal Church International according to the *Manual*.

   _____

   _____

   _____

   _____

4. State the objective of the United Pentecostal Church International in organizing Global Missions. _____

   _____

   _____

   _____

5. What is the message of Mark 16:15?

_____

_____

_____

6. What are the three basic characteristics of an indigenous church?
    A. _____
    B. _____
    C. _____

7. What is the ultimate goal and aim of the United Pentecostal Church International? _____

_____

_____

_____

8. What is the fundamental doctrine that must be taught by every missionary of the United Pentecostal Church International? Why?

_____

_____

_____

_____

9. In your own words, state the five objectives of Global Missions.
    A. _____

    _____

    B. _____

    _____

    C. _____

    _____

    D. _____

    _____

    E. _____

    _____

10. Explain the following statement: "The whole gospel to the whole world by the world church."

_____

_____

_____

_____

_____

_____

_____

_____

Personal Study Notes

Lesson 12

What Is the Structure of Global Missions?

Key Verse

"And God hath set some in the church, first apostles, secondarily prophets, thirdly teachers, after that miracles, then gifts of healings, helps, governments, diversities of tongues" (I Corinthians 12:28).

Lesson Goal

To show the structure of Global Missions and to understand the daily operation of the division as well as the responsibilities of the administrative officers.

WHAT I HAVE LEARNED

In II Corinthian 12, Paul gave a beautiful analogy of the church as the body of Christ. Each individual, being a member of that body, served in different capacities. He opened this chapter with a clear identification of spiritual gifts and their operation in the church. He continued with the importance of unity in the body, concluding in verse 28 by mentioning ministerial gifts that God has placed in the church. Among these ministerial gifts are those of helps and governments. It is imperative that we understand that God established these gifts in the church and, no doubt, this was to fill a need.

A careful study of the New Testament church reveals three distinct reasons the church exists in the earth.

1. To worship God in spirit and in truth.
2. To edify and perfect the saints.
3. To evangelize the world.

Other functions, however, are necessary for the daily operation and continuation of the work of the church in the earth; these are called functions of auto-continuity. Some examples are the purchase of property, the construction and maintenance of buildings, finances, and administration. Paul stated, "God is not the author of confusion, but of peace, as in all churches of the saints" (I Corinthians 14:33). Therefore, we must approach this lesson with a sincere appreciation of the provision that God has made for His church by giving us the gifts of helps and governments for the purpose of administration.

With this in mind, we will now look at the structure of Global Missions of the United Pentecostal Church International as is given in the *Global Missions Manual*.

I. GLOBAL MISSIONS BOARD

The Global Missions Board (GMB) consists of the general director of Global Missions, the secretary of Global Missions, the director of promotion, the director of education and Associates In Missions, six regional directors, nine pastoral members, and two district Global Missions directors. The UPCI Board of General Presbyters appoints the pastoral members for a five-year term. The General Conference ratifies such appointments. The district Global Missions directors serve a two-year term.

The responsibilities of the Global Missions Board (GMB) include carrying out the foreign missions enterprise of the UPCI under the supervision of the General Conference and the General Board. The GMB is the immediate governing body of Global Missions and the foreign work of the organization. It is therefore responsible for all world missionary activities of the UPCI, both in the USA and on the various mission fields, in accordance with the Global Missions Policy (*UPCI Manual*, Article XII). It examines candidates and recommends appointments to foreign service. In judicial matters pertaining to global missionaries, the GMB serves in the capacity of the district board in the area of investigation.

The GMB meets three times each year to review the status of the division, deliberate, plan, and make decisions relative to major aspects of foreign ministry.

II. GLOBAL MISSIONS ADMINISTRATIVE COMMITTEE

The Global Missions Administrative Committee (GMAC) consists of four divisional executives: the general director of Global Missions, the secretary of Global Missions, the director of promotion, the director of Education/Associates in Missions, and six regional directors.

This committee has authority to act in all matters that do not specifically require action by the GMB. As all committee members are at World Evangelism Center (Hazelwood, Missouri, USA), the committee counsel is readily available for such decisions. This relieves much of the detail work of the GMB.

It also provides answers based on committee decision at the earliest possible moment without unduly placing responsibility upon any single member of the Global Missions executive staff.

A. General Director of Global Missions

The general director of Global Missions is the chair of the Global Missions Board. He chairs the GMB and serves on the UPCI's Board of General Presbyters and Executive Board. He strives to work in harmony with the general superintendent and all other divisional heads.

As the executive head of the GMB, the director gives spiritual and organizational leadership to this vast ministry at home (USA and Canada) and abroad. He seeks to coordinate the work of Global Missions with the total aspect of the general organization. In order to fulfill these duties, he must keep fully informed of every facet of this worldwide enterprise.

Global Missions policy requires the director to supervise the disbursement of all global missionary funds. Missionaries must seek his approval before entering into any project requiring such funds.

Prospective missionaries should correspond with him regarding their call and possible appointment. Missionary personnel on the field must keep him informed monthly of their activities. Prospective national missionaries should follow the guidelines set up within the region and correspond to their regional director and/or area coordinator.

B.   Secretary of Global Missions

The secretary of Global Missions serves as secretary to the GMB. He chronicles all decisions and sends a copy of such minutes to the members of the Executive Board and the GMB. He also keeps proper financial records of Global Missions.

The secretary oversees all financial aspects of the Partners In Missions program. He supervises the disbursement of funds as authorized by Global Missions policy, GMB, and GMAC; the preparation of necessary documents as required by the work; the processing of missionary applications; and fulfills such other duties as may be deemed necessary.

C.   Director of Promotion

The director of promotion is responsible for keeping the church in North America informed, challenged, and involved in fulfilling the Great Commission. His duties include coordinating the missionaries' deputational ministry and missionary conferences; promoting Faith Promise giving and Partners In Missions; coordinating all Global Missions activities at the General Conference; and serving as coordinator of the district Global Missions directors. The director of promotion is also responsible for editing the *OnSite* and providing material for the *Pentecostal Herald* and such other publications requiring Global Missions material originating at the divisional level.

D.   Director of Education/Associates In Missions

The director of Education/Associates In Missions coordinates the development and implementation of training programs for nationals and the ministry of the printed word abroad. His portfolio includes vernacular radio broadcasting abroad; the Associates In Missions program; the annual School of Missions; and Global Missions Seminars in North American Bible colleges. Fulfilling these responsibilities demands representation of this program in North America, occasional on-site assistance, the coordination of short-term personnel, and other activities related to these areas of missions concern.

III.   REGIONAL DIRECTORS

The global missionary fields are divided into six geographical regions. Upon recommendation of the GMB, the Board of General Presbyters appoints six regional directors, each one to serve one of the respective regions. The geographical regions are defined as follows: Asia, Pacific, Central America and the Caribbean, South America, Africa (south of the Sahara Desert), and Europe and the Middle East (including the countries of Africa bordering the Mediterranean Sea). The regional directors are appointed for a term of four years and are supported through the Partners In Missions plan, the same as missionaries. An informal summary of their responsibilities is as follows:

In North America the regional director seeks qualified candidates for his respective fields, represents his region to the GMB, spends two or three months per year promoting the missionary endeavor, promotes the needs of unevangelized territories within his region, and generally serves as a good-will ambassador. This is accomplished by representing the needs and burden of his region to the North American church.

While abroad, he supervises the works in his region under the jurisdiction of the GMB and the general director of Global Missions. He makes regular reports and recommendations to the GMB. It is his responsibility to represent the North American church to the global missionaries and the overseas church. He works to maintain harmony among all the brethren, to establish priorities within his region in cooperation with the missionaries, and may be called upon to settle problems that might arise. He is to promote world evangelism, the establishing of indigenous churches, encourage the training of national ministers, and generally work for the total fulfillment of the Great Commission in the area for which he is responsible. He also represents the national churches in his region to Global Missions and the North American church.

Regional directors sit in an advisory capacity with the Board of General Presbyters. They are members of the GMAC and GMB.

WHAT HAVE YOU LEARNED?

Give short answers to the following questions.

1. Why are the gifts of helps and governments necessary in the church?

2. List the members that comprise the Global Missions Board, UPCI.

3. Describe briefly the duties of the Global Missions Board.

4. List the four members that make up the Global Missions Administrative Committee.
   A. _____
   B. _____
   C. _____
   D. _____

5. What is the difference in the operation of the Global Missions Administrative Committee and the Global Missions Board?

6. Who chairs the meetings of the GMAC and the GMB?

7. What are the basic duties of the secretary of Global Missions?

_____

_____

_____

8. What are the basic duties of the director of promotions?

_____

_____

_____

9. Who has the responsibility and oversight of the Bible school training programs for all foreign fields? _____

_____

10. Name the six regions of the world as divided by Global Missions.
    A. _____
    B. _____
    C. _____
    D. _____
    E. _____
    F. _____

Personal Study Notes

Lesson 13

What Is the Missionary's Role in the National Church in Its Beginning?

Key Verse

"According to the grace of God which is given unto me, as a wise masterbuilder, I have laid the foundation, and another buildeth thereon. But let every man take heed how he buildeth thereupon" (I Corinthians 3:10).

Lesson Goal

To clarify the role of the missionary in the national church in its early stages of development as he sets the stage for its future growth and maturity as an indigenous church.

WHAT I HAVE LEARNED

The work of a land surveyor can be somewhat complicated at times depending on the circumstances involved. The quality of his finished work always depends upon the accuracy of his original point of reference and how true he has maintained his work from that point.

> The quality of the surveyor's finished work always depends
> upon the accuracy of his original point of reference and
> how true he has maintained his work from that point.

The Book of Acts continues to be the original point of reference for our study of world missions. It is there we find the birth, ministry, and expansion of the New Testament church. It is there that we find accurate references to the day-by-day activities and operation of the body of Christ in the earth. It is there, in Acts, that we find the needed blueprint for the work of world missions today. May the Lord help us to remain true to His plan in the establishment of His church!

I.   THE MISSIONARY AS FOUNDER

The words of the apostle Paul to the church he founded at Corinth reflect the duty and heart-felt responsibility of every pioneer missionary. This duty is to lay the foundation of the New Testament church in a far-off land, among people who speak a different language, follow different practices, and have different beliefs than those of his own. From the earliest days of his involvement in a foreign land, the missionary must begin the crucial work of establishing the foundation upon which the work will stand in years to come.

A.   The Right Place and the Correct Way to Start

After being sent out from Antioch on their first missionary journey, Barnabas and Saul arrived at Salamis and there they "preached the Word of God" to the people (Acts 13:5). The following verses report the first miracle wrought by the Lord by the hands of these missionaries. A sorcerer named Bar-jesus (Elymus) was stricken blind at the words of Paul. In Acts 14:7 when they arrived in Lycaonia, we are told, "And there they preached the gospel." Again, following the preaching of the Word, a miracle, the healing of a lame man, took place. This is in perfect harmony with the Great Commission as recorded in Mark 16:15-20. Jesus said that signs would follow those that believed and preached the gospel.

It is therefore important to understand that from the beginning of his arrival on foreign soil, the missionary is, first, a preacher of the gospel.

1.   Preacher of the Gospel

The preaching of the death, burial, and resurrection of Jesus Christ is indispensable. Acts 2:38 must be preached and taught as the only plan of salvation. The full deity of Jesus Christ must be taught according to the Scriptures. One Lord, one faith, one baptism, and one body of Christ—the church—must be deeply implanted into the hearts of the people. Faith in God and love of God and our fellow man must be preached and lived. This is the laying of the foundation. The missionary must not cut any corners! There are no shortcuts! He cannot assume that after preaching and teaching a few times on these and other vital subjects, that the message has been established. He must preach it and teach it; preach it and teach it; preach it and teach it; and then start over again and again.

2.   Church Planter

Second, the missionary is a church planter.

In the parable of the Sower, Jesus said the seed is the Word of God (Luke 8:11) and in yet another parable He said the field is the world (Matthew 13:38). Preaching the Word of God can aptly be compared to the plowing and planting of a field with the hope of a good harvest. The natural result of the preaching of the gospel in a new area should be the establishment of the New Testament church.

Paul said, "I have planted, Apollos watered; but God gave the increase" (I Corinthians 3:6). As we focus again on our original point of reference (Acts), we see that because of Paul's preaching, a group of believers with trained leaders capable of carrying on the work was formed into a local church. This is also the duty of the modern missionary. New Testament evangelism should have as its goal the establishment of the New Testament church.

As a church planter, the work of the missionary includes:

(1) Evangelizing the unconverted
(2) Teaching the converts and training national workers and leaders.

B.   Preparing for Future Growth and Development

The foundation of any building is not an end within itself. It is actually the preparation for future growth and development. The same is true with the establishment of the church. The future will depend upon the strength of the foundation. No matter how big and beautiful the building may be, if cracks appear in the walls, you know that there is a weakness somewhere in the foundation. The same is true in the church. If we want a strong church in the future, we must dig deep and lay a strong foundation at the beginning. One that will be able to support future progress. Paul said that we "are built upon the foundation of the apostles and prophets, Jesus Christ himself being the chief corner stone" (Ephesians 2:20). Jesus said, "Upon this rock I will build my church; and the gates of hell shall not prevail against it" (Matthew 16:18). That rock is His Word, the revelation of His identity.

C.   What the Foundation Should Look Like

In order to understand what the foundation should look like, we must go back to the Word of God. By reading and studying carefully the Great Commission along with Acts 2-10, one should get the picture. Simply stated, the foundation should look like the original plan if we have followed the instructions correctly.

> The foundation should look like the original plan.

If the original plan called for repentance, then repentance should be there. If the original plan called for baptism in Jesus' name, then it should be there. If the original plan called for receiving the Holy Ghost with the evidence of speaking with other tongues, then that should be present. If unity and brotherly love were in the plan, then they should be present in the foundation.

II.   THE MISSIONARY AS BUILDER

A missionary is not intended to be a permanent factor in the life of a foreign people. His work is to make Jesus Christ the permanent factor. He needs to pass on to others as quickly as he can. It is possible to center the work too much on the leader, in the money that he brings into the work, and in his own abilities. When this happens, the missionary becomes indispensable to the work. The nationals depend on him for everything. Consequently, they do not develop the initiative to shoulder their own responsibilities, and the work never reaches the state of maturity where it can be left without the supervision of the missionary. This is always an unfortunate situation.

> The true success of a missionary cannot necessarily
> be measured by his ministry while on the field,
> but rather after he has moved on to another.

The true success of a missionary cannot necessarily be measured by his ministry while on the field, but rather after he has moved on to another. If he has laid a proper foundation, centered the work on Jesus Christ and not himself, taught the nationals and allowed them to assume their responsibilities, then when the day comes for his departure, the work will stand firm and continue to grow and develop.

The missionary must have a clear concept of his work as a missionary. He must understand the transitory aspect of his ministry. This has appropriately been compared to the scaffolding used in the construction of a building. What would we think of a builder who insisted that the scaffolding remain in place permanently for fear that his building would collapse?

The scaffolding is not to be considered a permanent part of the building. Its purpose is to give the necessary support to hold the permanent materials in place and in form until they have gained the needed strength to stand alone. Once this goal has been reached, the scaffolding will be carefully and systematically removed and moved on to the next building site.

This example can aptly apply to the role of the missionary in the national church. Note that the use of the term *support* does not always refer to financial support. However, far too often, the development of the indigenous church has been hindered by the introduction of foreign funds into the structure of the work. The result has been that the people depend on the outside funds for the church's support and advancement.

This weakens the spiritual and moral fiber of the church, kills the initiative of the members, and dulls their sense of responsibility. The people must be trained in independence rather than dependence.

The missionary must therefore be as a wise master builder. He must:

- **Know when support is needed.**
  - Timing is of utmost importance.
  - Too early can spoil the people.
  - Too late can hinder growth.

- **Know what kind of support is needed.**
  - o Moral
  - o Spiritual
  - o Financial
- **Know how much support is needed.**
  - o Don't overdo it.
  - o Don't under do it.

And then he must:

- **Know when support can be removed.**
  - o Too early can be deadly.
  - o Too late can be crippling.
- **Know what support can be removed.**
  - o The moral and spiritual will be long lasting.
- **Know how to remove the support.**
  - o Carefully
  - o Wisely
  - o Systematically

Only by leading a life of daily prayer and consecration, and by being sensitive to the Holy Ghost, can the missionary understand how to accomplish this delicate part of the work.

He must maintain a close relationship with:
- The Lord.
- The people.
- The mission that he was sent to accomplish.

If he drifts out of focus in any of these relationships, he can easily make bad judgments that will cause delays in the progress and development of the national church.

A good missionary will keep in mind that he is not a permanent fixture in the national church. He may be the one who laid the foundation and even the one who labored to build thereon. Yet it may happen, for various reasons, that he is not able to stay on the field until the church has matured to the point that it can function without the help of a missionary. This would then require that another missionary come to continue the work of developing the indigenous national church. If the founding missionary has built the work by indigenous principles, then the one who follows will not have any problems continuing in the same direction.

Paul said, "As a wise masterbuilder, I have laid the foundation, and another buildeth thereon" (I Corinthians 3:10).

WHAT HAVE YOU LEARNED?

Give short answers to the following questions.

1. Identify the original point of reference for this study of Global Missions.

_____
_____
_____
_____

2. Describe the message, which must be at the foundation of the church.

_____
_____
_____
_____

3. What should the foundation look like?

_____
_____
_____

4. What is the deciding factor for the future growth and development of the church? _____

_____
_____
_____
_____
_____

5. What should be the natural result of the preaching of the gospel in a new area? Why? _____

_____

_____

_____

6. Name two important areas of the work of a missionary church planter.
   A. _____
   B. _____

7. Explain why the work of a missionary can be compared to the scaffolding of a building. _____

_____

_____

_____

8. Name some things that the missionary must know about support of the national church. _____

_____

_____

_____

9. Describe the threefold relationship that the missionary must maintain.

_____

_____

_____

10. If the founding missionary has not built on indigenous principles, what are some problems that the succeeding missionary may face?

_____

_____

_____

Lesson 14

What Is the Missionary's Role in the Indigenous Church?

Key Verse

"And when they had ordained them elders in every church, and had prayed with fasting, they commended them to the Lord, on whom they believed" (Acts 14:23).

Lesson Goal

To clarify the role of the missionary in the national church after it has reached a state of maturity, whereby it is self-propagating, self-governing, and self-supporting

WHAT I HAVE LEARNED

By keeping the goal of the indigenous church in view, the missionary should have no problem understanding that his role in the national church is temporary. The day will come when his presence will no longer be necessary if he has closely followed the plan of the New Testament church. As the national church develops and matures, the role of the missionary will gradually see some important changes. Certain aspects of his role will see little if any changes while others will take on a completely different face.

I.   THE MISSIONARY AND THE SELF-GOVERNING CHURCH

The role of the missionary in the self-governing church will have changed dramatically from that of the early stages of the national church. Perhaps in his early days of involvement, he made most decisions alone. But now few, if any, are made by him. His role will have changed from that of a strong voice setting policy to that of counselor or advisor. A good rule to follow is that a missionary should never hold a position that a national is able to fill.

> A good rule to follow is that a missionary should
> never hold a position that a national is able to fill.

Self-government promotes a sense of spiritual responsibility that will manifest itself in every other area of the indigenous church. Without self-government, it will be difficult for the church to attain a state of self-propagation and self-support.

From the beginning, the missionary will need to pay close attention to those nationals who show leadership abilities. These men will likely become future leaders in the church, and the missionary should not hesitate to delegate responsibilities to them. Then they must be given the authority and the opportunity to carry out those responsibilities. One does not learn the art of driving an automobile by sitting in the backseat all of the time. There is, of course, a necessary time in the classroom and a time to sit beside an experienced driver observing his actions. But one has to get the feel of the steering wheel, the accelerator pedal, and the brake pedal, and that only comes by sitting in the driver's seat. This same principle is applicable to the church.

> God will always raise up capable men to match
> the needs of His church in any generation.

God will always raise up capable men to match the needs of His church in any generation. This is true regardless of location, culture, or tradition. Whether in a city of North America or in a village somewhere in South America or city in Eastern Europe, God will always have a certain man for a certain task at a certain time in His kingdom.

These men may not measure up to all of the personal desires of the missionary, and they should not be required to do so. The missionary must keep in mind that he is not there to change the culture but rather to establish the New Testament church. The missionary should give leadership training top priority in order to equip these men to do the work efficiently. Mistakes will be made. However, valuable experience will be gained. At times, the missionary may even find it necessary to allow the maturing leaders to make some mistakes in order to avoid the risk of greater errors in the future. (People learn from mistakes.)

At all times and in all things, the Spirit of God must direct every decision and action. A spiritual atmosphere of love, hope, patience, faith, and trust must be cultivated between the missionary and the nationals. This is the breeding ground of success in the national church.

In Acts 14:23 we see that "when they had ordained them elders in every church, and had prayed with fasting, they commended them to the Lord, on whom they believed." Paul and Barnabas realized that God had raised up certain men for certain tasks. After prayer and fasting, they placed these men into the Lord's hands.

They delegated the responsibility of the churches into their hands and believed that God was able to accomplish His will through them.

II. THE MISSIONARY AND THE SELF-PROPAGATING CHURCH

In the self-propagating church, the role of the missionary will change very little from that of his early days of involvement in the national church. He is still called of God, and he is responsible to preach the gospel to all men.

A. Practice Evangelism

The words of Jesus, "Go ye into all the world, and preach the gospel to every creature" (Mark 16:15), continue to apply to the ministry of the missionary in the indigenous church. Even though the national church may have well developed its ministry of evangelism under his leadership, evangelism should continue to occupy a position of top priority for the missionary personally. He must maintain a desire to see the lost saved and show this by his personal involvement in evangelism. He must keep the fire burning. It has often been said, "Action speaks louder than words." He will certainly not be able to be involved in every crusade or revival as he was in the early days, but his presence and his voice will be very encouraging and motivating whenever his involvement is possible.

B.   Promote Evangelism

In the indigenous church, the men and women that the missionary has patiently and lovingly worked with and ministered to, will continue to hold him in high esteem. They will respect his voice and confide in his counsel. Therefore, he should continue to promote evangelism as often as possible. This promotion of evangelism should be made at every level of the work, starting with the new convert. Every individual must be taught that he or she has a responsibility to reach lost souls.

The promotion of evangelism should also include creating opportunities for involvement. Making plans, setting goals, and following through with plans are important parts of an effective evangelism program for any national church.

Encouraging the planting of new churches is another important aspect of the promotion of evangelism. Until the New Testament church is established in every village, town, city, and neighborhood, the work of church planting is not finished.

C.   Teach Evangelism

The greatest change in the role of the missionary in the self-propagating church will be that the number of workers will have increased substantially, and he will be devoting a large portion of his time training them. This is nothing less than a God-given opportunity for the missionary to affect an entire nation. This is his opportunity to reproduce his burden and cast his vision to the national workers. The instruction of Paul to Timothy is worthy of mention here: "And the things that thou hast heard of me among many witnesses, the same commit thou to faithful men, who shall be able to teach others also" (II Timothy 2:2).

The possibility of reaching an entire nation with the gospel depends upon the degree of involvement of national workers in the task. The missionary must realize from the beginning that he cannot do it alone. Someone has said that it is better to put ten men to work than to do the work of ten men.

> It is better to put ten men to work than to do the work of ten men.

Sending out national evangelists as opposed to foreign ones has many advantages. The national evangelist will have no problem eating the food of his fellow citizens; he will adjust easily to the living conditions; he will understand the culture and traditions of his own people, and, perhaps most important, he will be able to speak their language and thus communicate the gospel to them.

III.   THE MISSIONARY AND THE SELF-SUPPORTING CHURCH

An ambassador from Ghana to the United States wrote concerning US Global Aid policy, "What Africa needs today is not someone who can give it fish to eat so it can ask for more fish each day. All Africa is asking for is a friend who can teach it to fish better so it can feed itself forever."

For the national church to reach a state of being self-supporting is actually not as difficult as it has been portrayed by some. Achieving this goal has two vital elements:

1. The biblical plan of tithes and offerings must be taught and practiced from the very beginning of every local church.
2. Faithful stewardship must be required on every level of the church.

If these two factors are in place, the national church should be self-supporting.

From the very beginning, the missionary should exercise wisdom and great care in involving foreign funds in the work. It is understood that some funds are necessary, but regrettably, the use of money by the missionary in the national church has often weakened rather than strengthened it. If the missionary were faced with the choice of too much money or too little money, it would probably be better for the national church if he chose too little money.

Following are some suggested guidelines for the missionary to follow:

1. No project should be started that cannot eventually be taken over, supported, and managed by the national church. One exception to this may be the Bible school. This is one area of the national work that can be greatly blessed by the proper use and management of foreign funds.

2. The national church should be required to participate in every project before involving foreign funds. Even though their participation may be small, it is extremely important.

3. It should be clearly understood that any and all foreign funds are limited and temporary. Great care should be taken because *temporary measures* can easily become *permanent policies* on the mission field. A good practice for the missionary to follow is to stipulate when and how it will end. It should always have an ending. This requires setting goals and guidelines and following through with them. It is always easier to extend the time limit of foreign support than to stop it.

4. Mission funds come from mission sources. Since the missionary is the one who is held responsible for such funds to those who gave them, he should maintain the control and oversight of how these funds are used.

5. The national leaders should have oversight as to how funds generated by the national church should be used.

6. For some time, the missionary may need to continue his help to the national church with the tasks of evangelizing new territories, the training of workers, and literature publication. However, the national church will eventually bear these responsibilities.

Someone said that God takes one day to grow a mushroom, yet He takes one hundred years to grow an oak tree. What kind of church are we trying to grow? *A mushroom church* or an *oak tree church?*

In his book *The Indigenous Church*, Melvin L. Hodges states:

"Anything which hinders the development of the church, no matter how much immediate good it does, should be sacrificed for the slower but more permanent good achieved through the establishment of the Indigenous church."[5]

---

[5] Melvin Hodges, *The Indigenous Church* (Springfield, Missouri: Gospel Publishing House, 1993), 117.

WHAT HAVE YOU LEARNED?

Give short answers to the following questions.

1. Why should a missionary not hold a position that a national is able to fill?

    _____

    _____

    _____

2. Should national leaders be required to measure up to the personal desires of the missionary? Explain. _____

    _____

    _____

    _____

3. Is it possible to benefit from mistakes that have been made? Explain.

    _____

    _____

    _____

4. Describe the atmosphere that must exist between the missionary and the nationals. _____

    _____

    _____

    _____

5. Why will the missionary's role have changed very little in the self-propagating church as compared to his early days of involvement with the work?

    _____

    _____

    _____

    _____

6. What are some important things to remember about the promotion of evangelism? _____

_____

_____

_____

7. Explain in your own words II Timothy 2:2.

_____

_____

_____

_____

8. Name the two necessary elements for achieving the goal of self-support in the national church.
   A. _____
   B. _____

9. Explain how the use of foreign funds in the national church by the missionary can weaken the church rather than strengthen it.

_____

_____

_____

_____

10. Describe the role of the missionary in the self-supporting church.

_____

_____

_____

_____

_____

Lesson 15

Keep the Main Thing
the Main Thing

Key Verse

"For what shall it profit a man, if he shall gain the whole world, and lose his own soul?" (Mark 8:36).

Lesson Goal

(1) To show that Satan causes confusion as to the true purpose of missions
(2) To help us maintain our focus on the salvation of souls

WHAT I HAVE LEARNED

INTRODUCTION: KEEPING PRIORITIES IN ORDER

The story is told of two vandals who broke into a large store in the night. The strange thing was that they did not steal anything. However, they changed many of the price tags on items in the store. On cheap items, they put high prices. On expensive items, they put cheap prices. In the morning confusion reigned. It did not take the storekeepers long to notice that the prices were wrong. Finally, the manager closed the store and spent the rest of the day putting things back in order.

In the same way, much needless delay in evangelism has been caused in the past fifty years. How? Simply by changing the price tags! The true value of the preaching of the gospel to the lost has been lost by placing more value on the social welfare of people than on salvation. Other programs and activities have replaced New Testament evangelism. Such programs focus more on the material and physical needs of humanity to the neglect of the spiritual.

T. F. Tenney, a former general director of Global Missions, wrote a book titled *The Main Thing Is to Keep the Main Thing the Main Thing*. Before Jesus ascended into Heaven from the Mount of Olives, He stated clearly what the "main thing" for His disciples and His church would be: "Go ye into all the world, and preach the gospel to every creature" (Mark 16:15). This one statement defines the mission of the whole church. It is a mission of going into the entire world in order to preach the gospel to all people everywhere.

In this lesson, we will consider four deceptions Satan uses to bring confusion and to change the focus of the church away from its true purpose.

I. DECEPTION NUMBER 1: "HOW CAN WE PREACH THE GOSPEL TO A MAN WITH AN EMPTY STOMACH?"

This deception has resulted in much mission resources being spent on social programs during the past century. But even worse, it has resulted in untold millions of lost souls plunging into an endless eternity hopelessly lost. Their stomachs may have been full but their souls were empty and void of the necessities of salvation. While it is true that helping to feed the hungry is a means by which one can show Christ-like compassion, this should never take the place of the preaching of the gospel. The condition of a man's stomach has nothing to do with the condition of his heart. Food may be the answer for an empty stomach, but only the gospel of Jesus Christ contains the remedy for a sin-filled heart.

> Food may be the answer for an empty stomach, but only the gospel of Jesus Christ contains the remedy for a sin-filled heart.

All men everywhere must hear and obey the gospel in order to be saved. A man with a full or empty stomach can hear, and by faith, repent and obey the gospel, and go to Heaven. On the other hand, this same man, if he has not heard and obeyed the gospel, will go to a devil's Hell, hopelessly lost, with a full or empty stomach.

II.   DECEPTION NUMBER 2: "HUMANITARIAN WORK IS THE MAIN WORK AND MISSION OF THE CHURCH."

Who would not be touched and moved with compassion at the sight of starving children or adults? We have all seen pictures and advertisements for various religious organizations as they make appeals for funds to feed and clothe the many unfortunate people in the world. It is certainly our Christian duty to do what we can to relieve the suffering of our fellow man. Too often this has been misinterpreted as missions work.

A national pastor gave the following testimony. He received the call of God to go to a particular village in a very remote farming region of the bush country of Togo, West Africa. Arriving in the village, he found the people very poor. They had few clothes and were hungry because of their extreme poverty. There were no churches, schools, or hospitals in the area. The villagers practiced the only religion they knew, that being their traditional forms of idolatry and voodoo. The pastor had nothing to give but the gospel. He began to teach and preach the gospel and the principles of the Word of God. The people received it gladly and put into practice the truths of the Bible. Many repented, were baptized in Jesus' name, and received the Holy Ghost.

After just two years, the results were amazing. Their fields, which were once barren, were now producing abundant crops. They built their own church building, complete with walls and roof. The people attending the church were now dressed modestly. The men wore shirts and ties; the women and children were neatly dressed as well. The joy of the Lord was evident among the villagers. The worship of the true God in spirit and truth had replaced the worship of idols What a change!

The interesting thing about this is that the area still has no schools or hospitals. And the village has only one church, an Apostolic church preaching and teaching the gospel of Jesus Christ. No program on the face of the earth has the power to transform the lives of miserable humankind like the New Testament plan of salvation. Christ died on the cross, was buried, and arose from the dead in glorious power. This must be preached everywhere. Because of the gospel, men and women have forgiveness through repentance, cleansing through baptism, and the power to overcome and be a witness through the gift of the Holy Ghost. That is grace! That is amazing grace!

Preaching, teaching, and reaching are priorities in missions work!

III. DECEPTION NUMBER 3: "SOCIAL WORK IN MISSIONS IS EQUAL TO THE PREACHING OF THE GOSPEL."

During His earthly ministry, Jesus gave the following reason for His coming: "For the Son of man is come to seek and to save that which was lost" (Luke 19:10).

When Jesus began His earthly ministry, He quoted the following verses of Scripture from the Old Testament prophet Isaiah (Isaiah 61:1-2).

"The Spirit of the Lord is upon me, because he hath anointed me to preach the gospel to the poor; he hath sent me to heal the brokenhearted, to preach deliverance to the captives, and recovering of sight to the blind, to set at liberty them that are bruised, to preach the acceptable year of the Lord" (Luke 4:18-19).

In this mission statement, Jesus did not establish social programs as the priority. Everything mentioned deals with the physical and spiritual needs of humanity, coupled with the fact that the remedy comes through preaching. This important declaration begins and ends on the same note: the preaching of the Word of God.

According to this prophecy, several benefits will result with the preaching of the gospel.

A. Preach the gospel to the poor

This is the first thing on the list. The results of social work may be a more comfortable life, but it does nothing for the inner needs of the soul. The preaching and practice of the Word of God releases the power of God to transform the entire life.

B. Heal the brokenhearted

Where is the social program that can heal the hurt of people in a war-torn nation? Or that can heal the deep wounds left by a divorce or abandonment by family? What can social programs do for the widow who is about to bury her dead son? What can Jesus do to heal these same situations? Everything! Through the preaching of the gospel, people are brought within reach of He who can do all things.

C.   Preach deliverance to the captives

Our world is full of spiritual captives. Men are captive to their own will, captive to materialism, captive to tradition, captive to sin, and held captive by the devil. Interestingly, this condition is not limited to the underprivileged people of the world. Deliverance comes through the preaching of the gospel. The gospel is a proclamation of liberty, like that given to Israel in Egypt and in Babylon.

D.   Recover sight to the blind

Bartimaeus (Mark 10:46-52) was healed when Jesus came within close proximity of where he was. As he cried out and reacted in faith, Jesus healed him. This is precisely what happens through the preaching of the gospel. Jesus is brought within reach of those who hear, and when they believe and react in faith, they will experience His transforming power.

E.   Set at liberty them that are bruised

Social programs have their place but should never be allowed to take preeminence over the preaching of the gospel. Social work is an act of charity and compassion but neither of these can set a man free from his misery and pain. Jesus said, "And ye shall know the truth, and the truth shall make you free" (John 8:32).

In Acts 8:5 Philip went down to Samaria to preach. It was a simple gospel message. The verses that follow tell about the miracles that took place as a result. "For unclean spirits, crying with loud voice, came out of many that were possessed with them: and many taken with palsies, and that were lame, were healed" (Acts 8:7).

F.   Preach the acceptable year of the Lord

Reference is made here to the year of jubilee as found in Leviticus 25:8-13. This was the year of release or *jubilee*. This was to be an acceptable year to servants who were then set at liberty, to debtors against whom all actions were dropped, and to those who had mortgaged their lands, for in this year the lands were returned to them. This *jubilee trumpet* was and is to be sounded by the preaching of the gospel. Paul referred to this same subject as follows: "For he saith, I have heard thee in a time accepted, and in the day of salvation have I succoured thee: behold, now is the accepted time; behold, now is the day of salvation" (II Corinthians 6:2).

> Nothing can take the place of the preaching of the gospel.

IV. DECEPTION NUMBER 4: "THEY WILL NOT LISTEN TO THE GOSPEL UNLESS WE OFFER THEM SOMETHING ELSE FIRST."

It is good to give food, clothes, and money to the poor when you have such things to give. However, these things should never be given to induce people to come to Jesus Christ. Jesus Himself loved and helped the poor but most of His time was spent teaching, preaching, and making disciples. He knew at times that the multitudes followed Him not just because of the miracles, but also for the loaves and fishes (John 6).

> If material gifts could save lost souls, the entire world would have been converted long ago.

Gifts of food, clothing, and money can never bring the same results as the Word of God and the Holy Spirit. Perhaps the giving of food will save a man from dying of starvation, medical aid can fight disease, building houses can make life more comfortable, but poverty and sickness are not the root causes of this world's misery and suffering. At the root of this world's woes is sin, and only the gospel of Jesus Christ has the remedy for sin.

The early church was a church of compassion. It took care of those in need within the church—especially the widows. Paul instructed, "As we have therefore opportunity, let us do good unto all men, especially unto them who are of the household of faith" (Galatians 6:10). We do have a responsibility to others, especially to our brothers and sisters in the faith who are in need.

We are to have the same compassion that Jesus showed. If there is a natural disaster causing starvation in a poor country, we as a church should be the first in helping. If God has blessed us with material goods, we should share it with the needy. However, the greatest exhibit of compassion is the sharing of the gospel, which can change all aspects of that country.

Gifts of food, clothing, and money may draw a crowd, but only the gospel introduces the sinner to Jesus Christ, the Savior. When Peter and John encountered the lame beggar at the Beautiful Gate of the Temple, Peter's words were, "Silver and gold have I none; but such as I have give I thee: In the name of Jesus Christ of Nazareth rise up and walk" (Acts 3:6).

V.   WHAT IS THE VALUE OF ONE SOUL?

In closing this lesson, let us consider the value of a soul in order to better understand the value of the preaching of the gospel.

Jesus asked the question, "For what shall it profit a man, if he shall gain the whole world, and lose his own soul?" (Mark 8:36). Here, Jesus spoke of one soul, "a man." He simply said that if a man were to gain all the wealth, land, houses, cars, or clothes of this world and then lose his soul, all would be in vain. Therefore, we see that it is impossible to estimate the value of one soul by measures of this world's goods. But the true value of one soul can be seen in the fact that Jesus Christ shed His precious blood to redeem that soul from eternal destruction (I Peter 1:18-19) Therefore, we must go, we must preach, and we will reach the lost. Why does Satan want to confuse the focus of the church? He wants to hinder the preaching of the gospel of Jesus Christ.

Paul said, "If our gospel be hid, it is hid to them that are lost: In whom the god of this world hath blinded the minds of them which believe not, lest the light of the glorious gospel of Christ, who is the image of God, should shine unto them" (II Corinthians 4:3-4). Simply stated, if they do not hear, they cannot believe and be saved.

> Simply stated, if they do not hear, they cannot believe and be saved.

WHAT HAVE YOU LEARNED?

Give short answers to the following questions.

1. Define the mission of the church in one statement.

    _____
    _____
    _____

2. State the four deceptions that Satan attempts to spread into missions work.
    A. _____
    B. _____
    C. _____
    D. _____

3. What is the ultimate purpose of these deceptions?

    _____
    _____
    _____

4. Should missions work be involved with the feeding of the hungry? When and how? _____

    _____
    _____

5. Can the needs of people be met through the preaching of the gospel? How?

    _____
    _____
    _____

6. From Luke 4:18-19, list the six areas of ministry mentioned by Jesus.
    A. _____
    B. _____
    C. _____
    D. _____
    E. _____
    F. _____

7. What is meant by "preach the acceptable year of the Lord"?

    _____

    _____

    _____

8. What is at the very root of this world's misery and suffering and how must it
    be dealt with? _____

    _____

    _____

    _____

9. Why did the multitudes follow Jesus during His ministry on earth?

    _____

    _____

    _____

10. Explain the value of a soul.

    _____

    _____

    _____

    _____

Personal Study Notes

Lesson 16

Tactics Satan Uses to Keep Missions off Balance

Key Verse

"Lest Satan should get an advantage of us: for we are not ignorant of his devices" (II Corinthians 2:11).

Lesson Goal

To reveal the tactics of Satan in hindering the growth and development of the national church and to understand the serious consequences of these deceptions

WHAT I HAVE LEARNED

I.   DEPENDENCE ON THE MISSIONARY

What would you think of an eight-year-old child that does not attempt to walk but rather insists on being carried everywhere on its mother's back? Or what would you think of a mother who refuses to allow her eight-year-old child to walk on his own but insists on carrying the child herself? Even though these examples do not sound reasonable, both could be aptly applied to some relationships between national churches and missionaries. Early in the life of a child, the mother must begin to allow and encourage her child to stand alone and to take those first steps. She knows there will be many falls before the art of walking has been mastered. Yet because of her love for the child and her concern for the future of the child, the wise mother will carefully and systematically withdraw her physical support.

This same principle is true for every national church on the mission field. It must be remembered that the missionary should not be considered the "Papa" of the nationals. Obviously, this will lead to a wrong concept. Many cultures look upon the father as being responsible to provide for his children until his old age and death.

However, it is altogether proper to allow the mother-daughter concept in the church as this is more in line with the model of the Book-of-Acts church. For example, the church at Jerusalem could easily be considered as the mother church from which other daughter churches were established. When problems arose, they were brought to Jerusalem for a final judgment (Acts 15:1-31).

Unfortunately, Satan has hindered the growth and maturity of many national churches by convincing nationals to depend on the missionary for many unnecessary things. A missionary cannot do for the national church what the national church should be doing for itself. On the other hand, some missionaries who have overly enjoyed the feeling of being in control have helped to create this kind of atmosphere. Both actions are out of context with New Testament church principles and therefore should be stopped and avoided in the future.

II.   DEPENDENCE ON FOREIGN SUPPORT

Jesus said, "Upon this rock I will build my church; and the gates of hell shall not prevail against it" (Matthew 16:18). Regardless of the culture, race, or nationality, wherever the gospel is preached and practiced, it will produce a church that has the potential to reproduce, govern, and support itself. Satan fears such a church!

This trick of Satan has prevented the blessings of God from coming into many national churches. Many references in the Bible clearly speak of the promised blessings of God to those who give to and support the work of His church in the earth.

- ". . . a blessing, that there shall not be room enough to receive it" (Malachi 3:10).

- "Give, and it shall be given unto you; good measure, pressed down, and shaken together, and running over, shall men give into your bosom" (Luke 6:38).
- "It is more blessed to give than to receive" (Acts 20:35).
- "God loveth a cheerful giver" (II Corinthians 9:7).
- "But seek ye first the kingdom of God, and his righteousness; and all these things shall be added unto you" (Matthew 6:33).

Failure to act upon these scriptural principles can be viewed as an act of doubt or an act of rebellion, both of which are sin. God's plan for His church is such that if the people will obey the principles of His Word in giving, He will bless them in ways that will surpass their imagination. In simple terms, when His principles are practiced, His promises will be accomplished!

When His principles are practiced,
His promises will be accomplished!

God blesses the one that gives. This is why the Lord has abundantly blessed the North American church. She has consistently given through the years for the advancement of the kingdom of God in the earth. However, it must be understood that this is not a special favor that God has granted, but rather in keeping with the promise of His Word. He will do the same thing in any nation and among any ethnic group.

We now understand why Satan strives to deceive a national church into depending too much on foreign funds rather than giving and sacrificing for its own support. Not only does this prevent the blessings of God, but it also prevents the progress of the church. Foreign funds are always limited, but God's funds are unlimited. If the national church depends too much upon foreign funds, its growth and development will be limited. However, if it depends upon God and practices His plan, its growth and development will never be limited.

Every national church must be trained in independence and not dependence. The use of the term *independence* does not in any way imply isolation. Nor does it mean to encourage a spirit of independence that seeks to operate separate and apart from the organization. Rather, it means a church that is independent in the sense that it does not depend upon foreign funds or personnel for its existence or for its continued advancement and growth.

III. THE MISSIONARY DOING THE WORK OF NATIONALS

As the early church began to grow, the ministering to the needs of the people became an increasingly large task. This moved the apostles to make the following decision: "It is not reason that we should leave the word of God, and serve tables" (Acts 6:2). This of course led to the choosing of deacons to fulfill this needed ministry of service. The necessity of this ministry was never a question, but rather a question of priorities. The apostles said, "We will give ourselves continually to prayer, and to the ministry of the word" (Acts 6:4).

As we discover tactics used by Satan to keep the work of missions off balance, let us consider the importance of setting and following priorities by the missionary. His work of preaching, teaching, and training is of such eternal importance that he cannot afford to be sidetracked. Time is one of his most valuable assets. Wise use of time in the work of missions means, "souls saved or lost." The missionary must therefore use his time in the most efficient way possible to accomplish his mission.

When missionaries consider the needs among the people to whom they have been sent, it is like looking up into the sky at night and viewing the innumerable stars. They must therefore be able to maintain their focus on the mission as a whole. That is the *"Big Picture"* or simply their purpose of being on the field. Satan will attempt to frustrate their purpose by occupying their time in many needful areas of ministry that actually should be carried out by the nationals.

The following are some areas of ministry that the missionary will be involved with on the field. The mention of these activities is not in any way intended to diminish their importance, but rather to place emphasis on the prioritized work of the missionary.

A. Baptism of Converts

Certainly, nothing is wrong with the missionary baptizing new converts. In fact, this is in fulfillment of the Great Commission. In the early stages of the national church, the missionary may find it necessary to help regularly with the baptism of converts. However, as pastors are trained and the church matures, this task should be turned over completely to the pastors. Why? Because a spiritual relationship is established between a convert and her pastor when she is baptized in Jesus' name for the remission of sins.

It is similar to the relationship that is established at birth when a newborn child is placed in its mother's arms. The newborn begins immediately to learn her mother's voice and touch. The same is true with new converts. They should begin to learn immediately the voice and touch of the man of God who baptized them in Jesus' name. This is the beginning of a spiritual relationship that is intended to last for life. Satan will work diligently to prevent this relationship from being established.

Paul explained in I Corinthians 1:13-16 that his principle objective was to preach the gospel. He was not attempting to diminish the importance of baptism but rather to emphasize the more important task of preaching the gospel. Paul evidently delegated the work of baptism to the local pastors and workers in order to give his full time to more important things.

B.   Weddings, Funerals, and Baby Dedications

Again these special ceremonies will be remembered for years to come by those involved. This is a wonderful opportunity for a pastor to make a lasting impression on individuals, families, and entire communities. Many will be the times that the missionary will be invited to attend and officiate at these events. However, he would be wise to turn these responsibilities over to local pastors for obvious reasons, one of which is to encourage the people to look to their pastors for spiritual guidance and to allow the pastors to feel their responsibilities toward their people.

Remember, the missionary's involvement in the national church is temporary, no matter for how long a time that may be. But the national pastor will be there when the missionary has moved on to other fields of labor.

C.   Filling Leadership Positions

As has been already mentioned in a previous lesson, the missionary should not fill any position in the national church that a national can fill. Rarely should the missionary accept the responsibility to pastor a local church and that only briefly until a national pastor can be installed. Teaching in the Bible school is one of the most influential activities for the missionary. This may as well be the one area of his longest involvement in the national church. But again, as soon as possible, this task should be turned over to competent and qualified nationals.

The missionary should not fall into the trap of feeling it necessary to put his hand on everything that is done. Nor should he allow himself to make every decision concerning the work. He must learn the valuable art of self-discipline and practice it. He is only one man and can only do the work of one man himself. But by training others and then delegating the work to others, he will find it possible to accomplish much more. And in doing so, he will also be constantly working toward an indigenous national church.

D. Disciplining Members

This can be a very delicate work even in the best of situations. The missionary is already a stranger among a people whose culture is different from his own. Therefore, any measure of discipline handed down by the missionary will usually be viewed as unfavorable. He will be accused of not understanding the customs, traditions, and feelings of the nationals.

It may be necessary at times, because of his position on the national board, for the missionary to be involved with the decision of discipline for a pastor who has sinned. Nevertheless, even in this case, the national brethren should pass along the final decision.

The matter of discipline of church members is a necessary part of self-government of a local church. While a local pastor may call upon the missionary for counsel, the missionary should avoid any direct involvement in the disciplining of members.

Jesus said, "The thief cometh not, but for to steal, and to kill, and to destroy" (John 10:10). One precious commodity that Satan seeks to steal is the time of the missionary.

IV. THE MISSIONARY TRYING TO WESTERNIZE INSTEAD OF EVANGELIZE

Quite often the missionary falls into a trap of frustration because, without realizing it, he measures the progress of the national church by the church in his homeland. While this may be a natural tendency, it should be avoided at all times. This trap of frustration has a twofold effect. Not only is the missionary affected, but the nationals as well will experience frustrations if they feel that they are not measuring up to the requirements of their missionary who is trying to impose foreign customs upon them.

Jesus did not say, "upon this rock I will build my American/European/African/Asian, and so forth church." He did say, however, "my church." The preaching and practice of the gospel will produce the New Testament church, and some common results should be expected. While the results may be the same whether in America, Europe, Africa, or Asia, the reaction to the gospel may differ from one culture to another. For example:

A.   Common Results

The preaching of repentance will produce repentance among those who hear. Preaching baptism will result in people being baptized. And the preaching of the promise of the Holy Ghost will result in people receiving the Holy Ghost.

B.   Different Reactions

American-style worship may come naturally to an American but it will seem very strange to an Asian. On the other hand, the Asian way of worship is unique and beautiful to the Asian but may seem unusual to the western mind. Who is right? Who is wrong? The answer is that both are right and neither is wrong. God is looking for true worshipers that worship Him in spirit and truth. True worship is spontaneous and voluntary. It may take on a different look depending upon the people and culture involved. It is quite natural for the Guatemalan church to take on a Guatemalan appearance, the Indian church to look Indian, or the Congolese church to reflect Congolese culture.

The issue here is not doctrinal matters or matters pertaining to biblical principles. The Word of God is forever settled in Heaven and must not be added to or taken away from. We must preach it and not seek to change it.

The wise missionary learns to present the gospel as the water of life to the nationals in their own cup and not in a foreign one. This simply means he must learn the art of communication with the people to whom he has been sent. This is more than just learning their language; it is praying and allowing the Lord to work through him to make contact with the people on their level. The missionary will do well to include in his daily prayers, a request to the Lord to help him better understand the people and their needs, and then to watch and listen closely to them. He will learn many valuable lessons in observing the simple, daily life of the people after having prayed for understanding.

V. PUTTING EMPHASIS ON SOCIAL PROGRAMS RATHER THAN EVANGELISM

One of the strongest motivations for social programs is compassion for those who are underprivileged and in need. As important as this may be in most countries, these efforts should grow out of the local church. The local church, the body of Christ, is God's tool for Christian caring and sharing. Therefore, all acts of compassion should be channeled through the local church in order to encourage the people in the area to see the church as a city of refuge in times of trouble. Yet in doing so, great care must be taken not to allow social welfare to become the major emphasis of the church. At all times and in all ways, the major emphasis of the church must be evangelism.

The following comparison will help us to see and better understand the importance of the work of evangelism in Global Missions.

Social Programs	Evangelism
Backed by human ability	Backed by the power of God
Formulated by man	Planned and ordained by God
Please men	Pleases God and men
Relieve temporary misery	Delivers from eternal destruction
Change the exterior appearance of man	Changes the interior condition of man
Bring hope of a better life on earth which is temporary	Brings hope of a better life in Heaven that is eternal.
May save lives	Saves souls

Paul stated clearly his purpose as an apostle and missionary to the Gentiles in the following verse: "Unto me, who am less than the least of all saints, is this grace given, that I should preach among the Gentiles the unsearchable riches of Christ" (Ephesians 3:8). At best social programs are limited. But what did Paul say? He said, "The unsearchable riches of Christ."

Let us look once again into the Book of Acts to see the value of evangelism as opposed to social programs and other such activities: "Then Philip went down to the city of Samaria, and preached Christ unto them. Moreover, the people with one accord gave heed unto those things which Philip spake, hearing and seeing the miracles which he did. For unclean spirits, crying with loud voice, came out of many that were possessed with them: and many taken with palsies, and that were lame, were healed. And there was great joy in that city" (Acts 8:5-8). At best, social programs produce happiness, but the result of New Testament evangelism is *great joy.*

WHAT HAVE YOU LEARNED?

Give short answers to the following questions.

1. Explain the mother-daughter concept of the New Testament church.

   _____
   _____
   _____
   _____

2. How does depending on foreign support hinder the work of missions?

   _____
   _____
   _____
   _____

3. Why has God blessed the North American church?

   _____
   _____
   _____
   _____

4. What happened in Acts 6:1-7? Why?

   _____
   _____
   _____
   _____

5. Why is time one of the missionary's most valuable assets?

   _____
   _____

6. Why should the missionary leave the tasks of baptisms, weddings, funerals, and so forth to the national pastors? _____

_____

_____

_____

7. What is a good rule for the missionary to follow concerning leadership positions in the national church? _____

_____

_____

_____

8. What are some common results of the preaching of the gospel regardless of the culture? _____

_____

_____

_____

9. In what ways may cultural differences affect the church?

_____

_____

_____

10. What are the unsearchable riches of Christ? _____

_____

_____

_____

Lesson 17

The Missionary as a Steward

Key Verse

"Let a man so account of us, as of the ministers of Christ, and stewards of the mysteries of God. Moreover it is required in stewards, that a man be found faithful" (I Corinthians 4:1-2).

Lesson Goal

To see and understand the responsibility of the missionary as a steward and the importance of his faithful accountability to God, to the sending churches, and to the organization

WHAT I HAVE LEARNED

The key word here is *faithful* in the sense of being trustworthy. If you put any other word in its place, the value of stewardship is lost. The word *steward* literally means "manager or overseer of another person's wealth, gifts, and possessions."

The words of Jesus, "Well done, thou good and faithful servant" (Matthew 25:21, 23), have become synonymous with the teaching of Christian stewardship, and rightfully so. Matthew 25:21, 23 uses the word *faithful* four times. Again in Luke 16:10-12, the parable of the unjust steward mentions the word *faithful* four times. In the teachings of Jesus, faithfulness was always rewarded and unfaithfulness always punished.

In his epistles, Paul spoke of being "found faithful" (I Corinthians 4:2); "faithful in the Lord" (I Corinthians 4:17); being a "faithful minister" (Ephesians 6:21); being "faithful brethren" (Colossians 1:2); being "counted faithful" (I Timothy 1:12); "faithful in all things" (I Timothy 3:11); being "faithful men" (II Timothy 2:2); "abiding faithful" (II Timothy 2:13); and even of having "faithful children" (Titus 1:6). John recorded the closing message to the church in Smyrna by saying, "Be thou faithful unto death, and I will give thee a crown of life." (Revelation 2:10).

Consider also that a minister, as the steward of God, must be blameless or above reproach. Look carefully at Titus 1:7 in the light of the following three versions of the Bible:

- "For a bishop must be blameless, as the steward of God" (KJV)
- "For the overseer must be above reproach as God's steward" (NASB).
- "Since an overseer is entrusted with God's work, he must be blameless" (NIV)

Paul also mentioned another important quality that must be present in the life of a steward, and that is honesty. "Providing for honest things, not only in the sight of the Lord, but also in the sight of men" (II Corinthians 8:21).

Keeping in mind these vital characteristics of faithfulness, blamelessness, and honesty, let us now look at some areas of ministry where the missionary must maintain an unquestionable practice of Christian stewardship.

I. FINANCES

A. Accountability

The missionary's accountability can be seen as twofold:

- He represents and seeks to fulfill the burden, desire, and sacrifice of the sending churches and organization to reach the world. They gave and sacrificed making it possible for him to be on the field. He is therefore accountable to them.
- He seeks to fulfill a calling to go into the entire world to preach and teach the gospel to all men. It was God who called him and God who worked through local churches to send him. He is therefore accountable to God.

The sobering call of the rich man to his unjust steward in Luke 16:2 was, "Give an account of thy stewardship." The lesson taught by Jesus in the parable of the Talents was accountability (Matthew 25:14-30). Paul stated clearly in Romans 14:12 that "every one of us shall give account of himself to God."

The best way to maintain an equitable form of accountability is through clear, precise, and regular reports. The missionary should be faithful with such reports to the churches and organization that supports him. A clear line of communication must be kept open and operating. A wise man will appreciate the fact that he must give account. Accountability makes a good watchdog!

B.   Honesty and Integrity

Honesty has a way of removing all fear from accountability. If an individual has properly used finances or materials that have been entrusted to him, he has no reason to fear giving account to others. On the other hand, dishonest practices give reason for fear of accountability.

Honesty has a way of removing all fear from accountability.

C.   Tithes

It is assumed that the missionary would have proven himself faithful in the area of tithing before going to the field. This certainly should be the case. A man who is not faithful in tithes and offerings in his homeland, cannot be trusted to be faithful in financial matters in a foreign land.

The missionary must be careful to maintain his practice of tithing on the mission field. Perhaps it would be easy for him to think that it does not matter in a foreign land where no one really knows what he does or does not do and therefore leave off the paying of his personal tithe. But never forget, God sees and knows all things and all men will give account to Him. Regardless of the system used for his personal compensation, the missionary must be faithful and honest with his tithe.

D.   Designated Offerings

These offerings are given and sent to the missionary to be used for special projects or needs on the mission field. These funds will usually be a specified amount for a specific purpose. Much care should be used in the handling of such funds. Once received, they must be guarded in security until the day of their use and then a clear, precise, and complete report made as to the disbursement of these funds. If there are funds remaining after the completion of the project, there should be some communication between the missionary and his overseers as to what will be done with the excess funds. It would not be wise for the missionary to assume that he is free to use these funds at his own discretion. He is the steward and not the owner of these funds.

The missionary is the steward and not the owner of these funds.

As a steward, the missionary must be wise and prudent in the use of all funds that he has received from all sources. In doing so, he will be in good standing with the churches and organization that sent him and with God who called him. He will also be setting a good example for the nationals and will be able to effectively teach them and require them to do the same.

E.   Property Management

One of the most important areas of involvement of the missionary on the field is that of teacher. Care should be taken to train the nationals in property management so that the investment of funds is not lost. Whether the funds come from foreign or national sources, this is of utmost importance for the continued development and security of the future of the national church. How sad it is, after people have given sacrificially, and a good parcel of land and/or buildings purchased, only to lose all because proper measures were not taken to obtain a clear set of documents showing ownership. Or, after having built a nice, attractive building, only to let it deteriorate after a few years because of the lack of simple maintenance practices such as painting and making needed repairs. These and many other costly mistakes can be completely avoided by properly training the nationals how to manage and maintain properties and facilities. This is practical Christian stewardship that should not be neglected.

II.   TIME

Jesus clearly referred to the importance of time in relation to the harvest when He said, "Say not ye, There are yet four months, and then cometh harvest? behold, I say unto you, Lift up your eyes, and look on the fields; for they are white already to harvest" (John 4:35). A sense of urgency can be detected in these words spoken by the Lord of the harvest. The hard labor of cultivating the ground, sowing the seed, and working in the field has produced its reward. There is a harvest in the field and it is ripe and ready to be gathered. But time must not be wasted.

Paul said, "See then that ye walk circumspectly, not as fools, but as wise, redeeming the time, because the days are evil" (Ephesians 5:15-16). And again, "Walk in wisdom toward them that are without, redeeming the time" (Colossians 4:5).

Minutes make hours, hours make days, days make weeks, weeks make months, and months make years. Therefore, if minutes are wasted eventually hours will be wasted. If hours are allowed to go by carelessly, before long it will turn into days, weeks, and months. It takes time to make disciples out of sinners. It takes time to establish a church. It takes time to teach and train pastors and ministers of the gospel. Therefore, souls saved or lost depend upon how wisely time is used. Proverbs 11:30 says, "he that winneth souls is wise."

The question may be asked, "Is the use of time actually a matter of stewardship?" In order to better understand this, consider the answer to the following question: Who has allotted the space of time to the individual and why or for what purpose? The answer is that God has given the space of time for reaching the lost and a steward is a manager or overseer of another person's wealth, gifts, and possessions.

So yes, the use of time is a matter of stewardship.

Efficiency is the key word here. The missionary should strive to be efficient in his use of time. The purpose of this lesson is not to give an in-depth study of time management, but we will mention seven simple guidelines that can be beneficial.

1. Identify the primary objective.
2. Analyze how time is spent.
3. Eliminate activities that waste time.
4. Identify proper priorities.
5. Delegate whenever possible.
6. Practice self-discipline.
7. Plan work schedules and calendars.

To the farmer, time means food. To the angler, time means fish. To the banker, time means money. However, to the missionary, time means a harvest of souls.

III. MINISTRY AND THE MYSTERIES OF GOD

"Let a man so account of us, as of the ministers of Christ, and stewards of the mysteries of God" (I Corinthians 4:1).

We are ministers of Christ and stewards of the mysteries of God. What are these mysteries spoken of by Paul and how are ministers of Christ stewards?

The mysteries, to name a few, are the Creation, the Incarnation, redemption, grace, the church, salvation, the Resurrection, eternal life, the return of Jesus Christ for His church, the judgment of all men, and eternity. Ministers of Christ are stewards of these mysteries according to what is done with the knowledge of these truths and how this is done.

A. Prayer

Consider that in the early church:

- Prayer preceded Pentecost.
- After prayer, the Word of God was spoken with boldness.
- Prayer preceded the baptism of the Holy Ghost.
- Angels were sent because of prayer.
- Prayer was made and the dead were raised.
- The sick were instantly healed through prayer.
- Because of prayer, prison doors were opened.
- Prayer always preceded ministry.

Pray because, "The effectual fervent prayer of a righteous man availeth much" (James 5:16). First Thessalonians 5:17 states, "Pray without ceasing." This simply means regularly, faithfully, and daily. Prayer helps to strengthen your faith: "Building up yourselves on your most holy faith, praying in the Holy Ghost" (Jude 20).

B. Study

Paul said to Timothy, "Study to shew thyself approved unto God, a workman that needeth not to be ashamed, rightly dividing the word of truth" (II Timothy 2:15). It matters very much how the Word of God is presented. This could be compared to the preparation of a meal. Using the best ingredients is important, but if they are not properly proportioned, they will not produce a savory meal. In the same way, the missionary must be well educated in the Word of God in order to preach or teach to the people what is needed in a timely and appropriate manner. That is "rightly dividing the word of truth." Studying is an essential part of preparation and preparation always precedes blessing. The time one spends in preparation by studying the Word of God is not wasted.

C.   Preaching/Teaching

A good rule for a minister of the gospel to follow throughout his ministry is: "Never be satisfied to give anything less than your very best."

> "Never be satisfied to give anything less than your very best."

Whether it is twenty or two hundred, because it is the Word of God, and because God sends him, the missionary should do his best to reach each one of them. Whether it is to kings and governors, to the educated or uneducated, to the rich or to the poor villagers, as a steward of God he should give his best without respect of persons (James 2:1-9).

Jesus Christ became the supreme sacrifice for the sins of the world. He was crucified, buried, and resurrected to accomplish the eternal purpose of God toward lost humanity. The missionary must exercise faithful and honest stewardship in the dispensing of these mysteries if he is to be found blameless before God.

WHAT HAVE YOU LEARNED?

Give short answers to the following questions.

1. What is the indispensable word in the practice of stewardship?

    _____

    _____

    _____

2. Name at least three essential characteristics of a good steward.
   A. _____
   B. _____
   C. _____

3. What are the two aspects of the missionary's accountability?
   A. _____
   B. _____

4. What is the best way to maintain an equitable form of accountability?

   _____
   _____
   _____

5. What is the best way to remove all fear of accountability?

   _____
   _____
   _____

6. How should the missionary handle all designated offerings?

   _____
   _____
   _____

7. Why is teaching in property management needed?

   _____
   _____
   _____

8. Explain the importance of time as relates to the harvest.

   _____
   _____
   _____

9. What is meant by "redeeming the time"?

_____

_____

_____

10. Name some helpful guidelines for efficient time management.

_____

_____

_____

_____

11. What are some things that will help the missionary exercise good stewardship as pertains to his ministry of the Word of God?

_____

_____

_____

_____

12. What is a good rule for a minister of the gospel to follow throughout his ministry? _____

_____

_____

_____

_____

Personal Study Notes

Lesson 18

A Full Circle of Missions

Key Verse

"Therefore said he unto them, The harvest truly is great, but the labourers are few: pray ye therefore the Lord of the harvest, that he would send forth labourers into his harvest" (Luke 10:2).

Lesson Goal

To focus our attention upon the need of national churches sending national missionaries into other nations, in order to multiply greatly the efforts of worldwide evangelism, and to fulfill the Great Commission of our Lord Jesus Christ

WHAT I HAVE LEARNED

A basic fact of life is that a healthy body has a God-given potential to reproduce itself. Consider also that the church, as the body of Christ by the indwelling of the Spirit of God, has this same God-given ability. Life begets life. And inasmuch as the Spirit of God is the source of all life, where His Spirit dwells is life and the potential to reproduce that life (John 1:4). This is true on the local as well as the national level. In fact, the goal of every local assembly and every national church organization should be to reproduce itself in another area or nation where the gospel has not been preached. In this lesson, our focus will be concentrated on the national level as we seek to understand the need of "a full circle" of missions work.

I.   WHY A FULL CIRCLE?

God never intended for the work of missions to stop until the return of Christ for His church. The apostle John saw an interesting sight in Revelation 7:9-10 that is relevant to this lesson: "After this I beheld, and, lo, a great multitude, which no man could number, of all nations, and kindreds, and people, and tongues, stood before the throne, and before the Lamb, clothed with white robes, and palms in their hands; and cried with a loud voice, saying, Salvation to our God which sitteth upon the throne, and unto the Lamb." By posing a few simple questions, we will see the importance of these verses in relation to Global Missions.

A.   Who are these people?

This is the raptured church clothed in righteousness and singing their songs of praise and victory before the throne of God.

B.   Where did they come from?

They came from every nation, every race, every tribe, and every language in the earth.

C.   Who preached the gospel to them?

The logical answer to this question would be those called and sent by God unto every nation, race, tribe, and language.

In the past, the work of missions was perceived as a straight line: Westerners being sent to the majority world. Considering that possibly fifteen thousand unreached people groups remain in the world, one can see this has been successful to a small degree in comparison to the overall population of the world. The concept of Westerners to the majority world is natural because these people come from nations where Christianity has dominated their culture throughout the centuries.

However, the world scene is changing rapidly. We are told that the largest Christian church in the world is not in the USA or Europe but in Seoul, Korea. It is estimated that at the turn of the century at least 60 percent of the world's Christian population will be located in majority-world countries. Statistics indicate that within the next few decades, the heaviest concentration of Christian population will have shifted to the African continent. Therefore, our concepts and methods of missions work must change in order to take advantage of these shifts if we are to reach the increasingly expanding population of this world. With the increasing worldwide Christian population, there should be a natural increase in the number of laborers called of God and equipped to go forth into the harvest. Our missions program must change from a "straight-line" concept to a 360 degree "full circle."

II.   A FULL CIRCLE: WHAT DOES IT LOOK LIKE?

A.   The 90-degree Missions Program

This has been the most commonly followed program through the years. The 90-degree program is that of sending out missionaries to a certain group of people to preach the gospel, convert them to Christianity, and to plant churches. This is in fact the first logical step in the fulfillment of the Great Commission. But too often, Christian missions organizations have remained on this level without going on to the next phase.

B.   The 180-degree Missions Program

At this level, the seed of the Word bears fruit. Nationals are trained, and in turn are reaching and pastoring their own people.

An evangelism program using the nationals and a training program has been incorporated.

Although the national church is beginning to govern itself somewhat, it is still under the supervision and care of the mission.

C.   The 270-degree Missions Program

The national church has now become nationalized and is taking care of its own needs. It has matured and is self-supporting. Through evangelism it is reproducing itself and has trained national leaders who are governing its own affairs. If the missionary is still there, he is usually involved with the Bible school and training program. The national church is growing and reaching into new regions but only within the borders of its own nation.

This admirable accomplishment is praiseworthy. Many national churches after years of existence never reach this state. However, at this point there is a need to take this church to the next level of development being the "full circle" of missions work.

D.   The 360-degree Missions Program

The "full circle" is accomplished when the national church, which was originally started as a missions church, gives birth to a mission of its own. The 270-degree position of missions work is desirable but often means that the national church has entered into a maintenance mode of just keeping itself alive. However, remember a healthy body will reproduce itself.

The 360-degree or "full circle" program not only maintains itself, but also generates other churches in other cultures. This simply means that the national church is sending or helping to send missionaries from their nation into other nations to preach the gospel and establish the New Testament church. The 360-degree church is a missions-minded church.

> The 360-degree church is a mission-minded church.

III.   ANTIOCH: THE MODEL OF A FULL CIRCLE

Once again, we will focus our attention on the model of the New Testament church at Antioch as is found in the Acts of the Apostles. Believers from Cyprus and Cyrene founded the church at Antioch as recorded in Acts 11. Luke mentioned the church frequently throughout the Book of Acts. Here are some important facts to remember about the church at Antioch:

- Antioch was the first church founded among the Gentiles. It was a multi-cultural church.
- The disciples were first called Christians at Antioch.
- Antioch was a spiritual church where the Holy Ghost could and did speak.
- It was from Antioch that the first missionaries were sent out. It was a missions-minded church.
- Antioch was a church that gave generously.

- Antioch was the place of departure of the *first, second, and third missionary journeys of Paul.*

Believers who scattered because of persecution evidently founded the church at Antioch as a missions endeavor among the Gentiles (Acts 11:19-30). This church quickly became a pillar and focal point of the truth among the Gentiles. By the time we reach Acts 13, the church dominated the scene as the launching pad for world missions. Paul based all of his missionary journeys from this church. Antioch quickly responded to the financial needs of the church at Jerusalem. It also seems that she, in some way, gave support to the early missionary efforts. The churches were established in Rome, Corinth, Galatia, and Ephesus. Churches were founded also among the Philippians, Colossians, and Thessalonians. Revelation mentions churches in Smyrna, Pergamos, Thyatira, Sardis, Philadelphia, and Laodicea.

In brief, Antioch was founded as a missions work but in time became involved in the sending of missionaries to preach the gospel and establish the church in the regions beyond. This represents a "full circle" of missions and this is what we should be striving for in every national church around the globe. Life gives birth to life and missions will give birth to missions.

IV.   A FULL CIRCLE. HOW?

Every true Christian is a member of the body of Christ and every local church represents the body of Christ in its locality. As Christians who have received the knowledge of the gospel, we are debtors to those who have not had this opportunity.

From the very beginning of a new church, the responsibilities of world evangelism must be taught to the converts. All believers must be made aware that they are debtors and should be taught how to discharge this responsibility. The task of world evangelism is too great to be limited to a select group of people from North America or Europe.

If this important mission is to be accomplished, it will be done by the vision and cooperative effort of every local church and every member.

When a church is founded, it must begin as a missions-minded church with a burden to reach other nations. Every pastor has the responsibility to penetrate his congregation with a vision for missions. This can be accomplished by sharing with them information from mission fields such as reports from missionaries, which can be received through the Global Missions. People informed will be people concerned. Every church should establish the practice of receiving regular missions offerings. Praying for missionaries and unevangelized nations should be given an important place in the local church. Jesus instructed His disciples in John 4:35 to "Lift up your eyes, and look on the fields; for they are white already to harvest." Looking at the conditions and needs of the foreign fields will help to create the needed burden and concern for the lost.

In brief, the "full circle" of missions can be accomplished in the church locally as well as nationally by regularly practicing these simple steps:

1. Teach missions.
2. Preach missions.
3. Give to missions.
4. Pray for missions.
5. Live missions.

WHAT HAVE YOU LEARNED?

Give short answers to the following questions.

1. Explain the basic principle of reproduction as it relates to the church and missions. _____

_____

_____

_____

2. What does the vision of John, found in Revelation 7:9-10, have to do with missions? _____

_____

_____

_____

3. In your own words, explain what is meant by a "full circle" of missions work.

4. Describe the following:

A. The "90-degree" missions program.

B. The "180-degree" missions program.

C. The "270-degree" missions program.

D. The "360-degree" missions program.

5. What is meant by the term "missions-minded church"?

6. Give some important facts about the church at Antioch.

7. Why do we say that Antioch represented a "full circle" of missions?

_____

_____

_____

8. Why do you think Paul based his missionary journeys from Antioch?

_____

_____

_____

9. What is the responsibility of the pastor of every local church to the congregation regarding world missions?

_____

_____

_____

10. What instructions did Jesus give in John 4:35?

_____

_____

_____

Missionary Spotlight
Frances Foster

By Dorsey Burk
Quotations from *Around the World with Jesus: The Frances Foster Story* by Frances Foster and Lynda Allison (an unpublished manuscript)

It must be that the Almighty God in the person of Jesus Christ had His great hand upon [my] life from the beginning. It is His compelling call that will never let go of the life truly committed to Him. Without Him, we can do nothing! Everything good accomplished is by His Spirit and must be for His glory. All He asks from us is a willing, yielded heart to do His will. Faith and obedience go hand in hand. Jesus said, "If any man will do his will, he shall know of the doctrine" (John 7:17). When we obey, even without a clear understanding, other Scriptures come alive to us, making the doctrine clear. How wonderful to be able to trust our loving, heavenly Father with our lives. — Frances Foster, c. 1990.

Frances Foster
December 1979

Frances Helen Foster, the fifth of eight children, was born November 10, 1920, into a devout Methodist family in Nyssa, Oregon, a "barren country infested only with jackrabbits, sagebrush, and dry alkali dust." Life was not easy in that eastern Oregon town in the Depression, but frugality and faith in God brought the family of Wilbur and Ruth Foster through. Frances stated, "We learned to trust God, work hard, and not to expect too much. . . . We learned to eat everything that was set before us and not to waste precious food."

Her dad's staunch holiness standards, learned from his Quaker parents, influenced the whole family. One night during a special evangelistic service when she was almost ten years old, God began to talk to Frances's heart. As the congregation was singing "Softly and Tenderly Jesus Is Calling," she made her way to the altar and repented. It seemed that from that early age Ruth recognized a special call on Frances's life.

After graduating from high school, Frances attended College of Idaho in Caldwell. When choosing a major for study, she informed the counselor that she wanted to prepare for missionary service as she felt God had called her to that kind of work. The counselor suggested that the teaching course would be basic preparation. Frances later stated, "Preparation was what I wanted, for in my heart was a burning desire to serve God with my whole heart and being. I felt I was ready for whatever God sent my way. But how little I really knew!" After transferring to Northwest Nazarene College and receiving her teaching certificate in 1942, Frances found herself teaching twelve students in grades one through eight in a one-room school in Deer Creek, Idaho, near Weisser.

Still feeling a need for more preparation for the mission field, Frances returned to college. She received her bachelor's degree in Christian Education from Westmont College, Santa Barbara, California, in 1946. She then took graduate courses at Multnomah School of the Bible, Portland, Oregon, and the School of Missionary Medicine at BIOLA in Los Angeles.

After graduating from Westmont, Frances joined the Christian Business Women to go out into rural areas of America and hold children's classes and adult evangelistic meetings for small churches with only one pastor for several towns. She boarded a train to Winona Lake, outside of Chicago, for a training session. On the train was an older man who started to pass out Christian tracts and asked to sit beside Frances. She told him about her call to India.

He surprised her by saying, "You need the Holy Ghost." The remaining conversation went like this:
"Holy Ghost? Oh, I already have the Holy Ghost."
"How do you know?"
"Because I have the witness that I am a child of God. Surely, I can't have God without having His Spirit too."
"Whatever you have of God is fine, but what you need is the Holy Ghost as the disciples received it on the Day of Pentecost."
Grover Fretwell proceeded to quote verses of Scripture to Frances all night. In response, Frances asked, "How do you do it?"
Fretwell's response, "But the Comforter, which is the Holy Ghost, whom the Father will send in my name, he shall teach you all things, and bring all

things to your remembrance, whatsoever I have said unto you" (John 14:26), stayed with Frances for the next five years.

After working with the Christian Business Women's youth/home missions endeavor for two years, Frances decided to go to Portland, Oregon. She worked at Emanuel Hospital. She stated, "Arriving in Portland, I found a place to stay near the hospital, where I worked as a nurse's aide from 3:00-11:00. The mornings were spent in prayer and Bible study, searching the Scriptures and seeking God's face for the Holy Spirit. When wondering about speaking in tongues, the Lord quickened the Scriptures in Isaiah 28:11 and 12 to me. . . . So tongues were even mentioned in the Old Testament." Frances received the Holy Ghost as a minister laid his hand on her head. She said, "As he laid his hand upon my head, I fell to the floor and a glorious light flooded my being, filling me with great joy and the assurance that the Son of Righteousness had filled my heart . . . . The Holy Spirit was like the bright noonday sun over me and I was enthralled with the presence of Jesus. He was so precious that I never cared about what was coming from my mouth."

Prompted by the Spirit, Frances contacted Grover Fretwell in Portland and told him about her Holy Ghost experience. He invited her and her friends to dinner and afterward emphasized the name of Jesus. He would later baptize her in Jesus' name in the Willamette River. When she came out of the water, Sister Fretwell gave a message in tongues, confirming that God was going to send her to many countries.

When Frances's plans to go to India in 1955 were put on hold because of a visa problem, a former missionary to India suggested that she could go as a tourist, spending six months in that land. Frances sought the Lord. "I asked Him what I could do to fulfill His call on my life. He gave me the most vivid vision I had ever had. I saw Mount Fujiyama in Japan as I had seen in pictures. The words followed: Japan, Hong Kong, Taiwan, Nepal, Pakistan, Italy, Holland, England, in successive order. He had given me all the countries that I should visit with the gospel message. I could feel His presence as He let me know that I should trust Him to open the doors and to supply all my needs. It was a walk of pure faith in His name."

Her first stop was Japan. She worked with missionary Eulalia Spoor, whom she first met at Multnomah School of the Bible. They rode bicycles to various preaching points as Frances learned to adapt to Japanese culture. Two months quickly passed by and it was time for her to fly to Calcutta (now known as Kolkata), India.

India was greatly different from Japan. The oppressive spirits, the swarming mass of people, the extreme poverty, and the strange smells assaulted her senses. She stayed with the Peters family, Anglo-Indians who pastored an English-speaking church, while she was in Calcutta. As she adjusted to India, God opened many other opportunities for Frances to minister in other areas of India. These opportunities caused Frances to experience the wide array of travel modes: rickshaws, overcrowded trains, raft-like ferries, rickety vans, taxis, horse-drawn carts, and so forth, as she traveled from Kashmir and Punjab in the far north, into Nepal, and then into southern India. Being able to tell the story of Jesus' love thrilled her soul and made all of the inconveniences bearable. Many people marveled that a single, American woman would travel alone. Of course, Frances knew she was not alone because Jesus went alongside and before her.

Frances stated, "New Year's Eve 1954 found me on a wide, rocking train from Madras to Kumbanad, South India. Perched on the baggage rack, I sang familiar Christmas carols, read from the Word of God and prayed with a group of Telegu-speaking girls on their way to camp. Six of them were 'Christians,' who wanted to hear more about Jesus, though they didn't know much English. We had a good time."

Finally, it was time for Frances to leave India and go on to Karachi, Pakistan. For six months in India she had traveled third class on the trains and lived under most strenuous and unsanitary conditions, but she never once had diarrhea or became seriously ill. However, during her final week in Bombay, while staying at the YMCA, she drank water the Y provided, thinking it had been boiled. By the time her plane landed in Pakistan, she was ill.

God allowed her to minister for a week in Pakistan and then it was time for her to move on to the Holy Land, Italy, the Netherlands, and England. All along the way, the Lord provided lodging, met all of her needs, and provided opportunities to share the Word. A short time later, she was back in Los Angeles, having traveled around the world by faith.

The trip around the world opened Frances's eyes, and she knew she would not be staying in North America. She received a letter from Eulalia Spoor, who wanted Frances to come and take her mission station. In September 1955, she bought a ship fare with the last $400 in her savings account and boarded the

Hikawa Maru bound for Japan. On board was another Jesus' name missionary couple who were on their way to work with Leonard Coote.

Frances gave herself diligently to language study and ministry. As an independent missionary, she had to depend on God to supply her needs. She often had to draw on the lessons she had learned about frugality and trusting God as a child. Although at times she was like the widow with the near-empty meal barrel and cruse of oil, God never failed to meet the needs.

Frances returned to America in 1960, but the pull of the lost world never left her. In late 1961, she returned to the mission field. She went to Japan and Hong Kong for a few months until she received a one-month tourist visa for India. She arrived back in Calcutta on February 26, 1962. Sister Amber, a friend and an inspector of schools, opened her home in Dharamsala to Frances. Frances traveled with Amber as she visited schools under her jurisdiction. Although she legally could not do so herself, Amber encouraged Frances to pass out tracts and talk to teachers and students about Jesus.

Frances was able to spend fifteen months in India on her one-month visa, as the government was so slow in declining her application for renewal. She arrived in West Pakistan on May 5, 1963. Frances wrote, "It was surely with mixed emotions, but with the assurance that God would lead this weary pilgrim, that I started out on a rickshaw with a bedding roll, a large metal box containing personal items, and my one suitcase to cross over into another strange land and situation. . . . Again, I was viewed with curiosity and distrust by other travelers. Where was I going? Whom would I meet there? These were all unanswered questions, which made me feel like Abraham must have felt as he made his first journey from Ur of the Chaldees."

Someone had given her the name of a professor who led a Pentecostal group in Lahore. He concluded that she was one of those "Jesus Only freaks." Nevertheless, he and his wife arranged for Frances to go to Murree Hills to study the Urdu language. Urdu was a completely different script from the Hindustani that she had been studying. She found the language difficult.

Eventually, God led Frances to Karachi, the nation's largest city. A. U. Alfred, who was stationed near Karachi in the Pakistani air force, asked her to come and hold meetings for a group that he led. He had already received the Holy Ghost in Peshawar while attending services conducted by a Spirit-filled missionary from England. Many in the group repented and received the Holy Ghost.

God also opened the door for Frances to minister in Mahmudabad, a very poor community of day laborers near Karachi. Living conditions were miserable. Water had to be carried from a long distance. God blessed the meetings with many miracles, healings, and deliverance from evil spirits. The crowds increased nightly until sometimes they estimated one thousand people crowded into the tent and surrounding area. The largest crowd was around seventeen hundred people. However, as Jesus' name was preached, leaders of the group decided Frances was a false teacher. After four months, it was time for Frances to move on.

A. U. Alfred invited Frances to go with him to his home village of Clarkabad in the Punjab. At one time Clarkabad had been a model Christian village. The Church of England founded Clarkabad primarily for Christians. The church invested much money in building schools, a seminary, a hospital, and so forth. However, the villagers were only Christians not born-again Christians and lacked commitment to the gospel.

Alfred and Frances received permission from the overseeing bishop to hold services in Clarkabad. The Lord began to work and hungry hearts began to repent of their sins and seek for the Holy Ghost. However, preaching about baptism in Jesus' name brought trouble.

By this time Frances had experienced several health problems and decided to return to America to renew her health. She departed from Karachi on May 25, 1964. In her first service back in Portland, she was healed of a heart condition. The doctor later confirmed, "Everything is fine, except for some intestinal 'bugs.' Some medication, good food, and care will renew your strength."

After caring for her parents who were injured in a car accident, Frances went to teach in a Christian school in Burbank, California. She taught thirty-three second graders for two years and then substituted the third year.

In June 1967, friends from the UPC of Burbank saw Frances board a ship in Long Beach to return to Pakistan via Japan. While in Japan, a lump in Frances's breast grew larger and more painful. After consulting with doctors at Kumamoto University Hospital, Frances decided to have surgery. Dr. Mori, to whom Frances had taught English years before, arranged for funds to cover the surgery and her recuperation.

Frances arrived back in Clarkabad the day before Easter in 1968. The village was experiencing revival. Brother Alfred had already baptized seventy people in Jesus' name in Clarkabad and more in other villages.

Soon after her return to Clarkabad, they heard of an Arthur Perry, who with his family was living in Karachi, working for a Canadian company. When his friends, George and Margaret Shalm, missionaries to India, visited the Perrys, Frances and Brother Alfred traveled to Karachi to visit them.

Frances stated:

I was not comfortable baptizing ministers. Brother Alfred, who had already baptized more than 200 people in Jesus' name, had not himself been baptized that way. Brother Shalm came to the rescue. After explaining the whole doctrine very nicely to Brother Alfred, who brought seven of his friend from that area, Brother Shalm baptized them in the lovely name of Jesus in the Indian Ocean near Karachi. That was a great day of rejoicing. Now they had not only more power, but also a greater understanding of this doctrine.

As the work continued to grow, so did the difficulties. Frances finally wrote to Reverend N. A. Urshan, the superintendent of the United Pentecostal Church International, asking for someone to come and help them. "Brother Urshan remembered having met me, and he really got busy to find us someone. The Everett Corcorans from Canada had wanted to go to India. Now they agreed to come to Pakistan. They would arrive in May of 1971."

The political situation in Pakistan was becoming increasingly tense as East Pakistan had declared its independence. With war seeming inevitable, Frances returned to America November 25, 1971, intending to join the fellowship of the United Pentecostal Church. She stated:

Feeling that I needed a better understanding of this Jesus Name message, I decided to attend Western Apostolic Bible College in Stockton, California. Brother Haney and all the staff were so kind to give me work to pay for my tuition. . . . I filled out all the application forms to be a missionary, but felt such an urgency to get back to the field. . . . that I agreed with Brother Scism and the others to return under an 'endorsement' plan. . . . By September of 1973, I had everything together and was again en route to Pakistan.

Revival continued to spread in Pakistan. Frances did her part by taking charge of the Sunday school department. She organized Sunday school seminars with officials from the UPCI headquarters in Hazelwood, Missouri, and taught teacher-training courses throughout the nation. As more churches were established, Frances encouraged the local congregations to have vacation Bible schools. Because of her efforts, many children received the Holy Ghost in their Sunday school classes and VBS.

Frances stated:

Teaching children has always been one of my priorities. I love it. It is so worthwhile to capture these young lives before they get into sinful habits. And we know that the children we teach today will be our church of tomorrow. We are already seeing that children we taught in the early days of Clarkabad and other places are becoming our pastors and leaders today.

Frances Foster received her full appointment as a United Pentecostal Church missionary in June 1976. She labored faithfully and was weary in body. She finally decided to heed the advice of some of the other missionaries and retire so she could have a long rest. In preparation for leaving for America in 1981, Frances "endeavored to visit all the Sunday schools to encourage the young pastors who had started new works and to leave as much visual aid material as possible."

Frances Foster returned to America with an uncertain future. Her life had been totally devoted to missions. How could she come home and simply warm a pew? She didn't. She taught English, loved and transported little children to church, and ministered in the Punjabi community in Kerman, California. She did what she knew best, and that was just do whatever was necessary and do it in the name of the Lord Jesus.

Then life took an amazing turn for Frances. At the age of seventy, she and Rev. Clarence Riddlesperger of Carmichael, California, united in marriage on December 29, 1990. On October 4, 2002, Frances went to be with her heavenly Bridegroom.

In 2014, the UPC of Pakistan reports a constituency of over 166,000 believers with nearly 3,300 churches and preaching points in a predominantly Muslim country.

Former regional director for Asia Garry Tracy wrote:

I first met Frances Foster in 1979 when my family arrived in Pakistan as missionaries. She was one impressive lady! Working in a predominantly Muslim nation as a single woman was no easy task. One could see immediately that Frances was totally committed to spreading the gospel to every person regardless of the cost.

Two years later, my family relocated to the area where Frances had been working for several years. We built a wonderful relationship, both personally and professionally. She was always respectful, willing to do whatever was required to move the work forward.

Frances excelled in evangelism and children's ministry. In those days ministry to children was not a priority for most but Sister Foster made it so. She was very effective in working with the national pastors and leaders to launch and expand effective ministry to children.

In evangelism, Frances was on fire for God and powerfully anointed. *Fearless* would be another word to describe her demeanor when challenged by a sometimes hostile environment. Pity the man or devil who tried to stop her from sharing the best news in the world with people who needed to hear!

Looking back, I wonder if my words of caution to her were lack of boldness on my part or words of wisdom. Her sacrificial spirit was equal to any in church history. Periodically, I noticed that she seemed to be short on funds to take care of herself or her humble residence. Upon probing further, I discovered that she had spent her personal money on some pressing need related to children's ministry or evangelism.

Thus, she was a wonderful true servant of the Lord doing all within her power with dedicated focus to save souls under adverse circumstances. Frances was an inspiration to all who knew her and loved her. There is no way to keep record of the thousands of lives—both children and adults—that entered the kingdom of God through the sacrificial ministry of Frances Foster.